Dedication

To those
who fulfill the principles of
Optimist International—
development of youth,
community, and one's self.

And to Don Salverda,
founder and first president
of the Roseville Area Optimist Club,
Roseville, Minnesota—
with gratitude for his
vision, leadership, generosity,
humor, and more.

Table of Contents

MEMBERS

Authors

Foreword

Cindra Kamphoff, Ph.D.

"A pessimist sees the difficulty in every opportunity. An optimist sees the opportunity in every difficulty." —Sir Winston Churchill

Not along ago, I was asked to deliver a talk to the Roseville Area Optimist Club. I said "yes" immediately. I couldn't wait. I was so excited to be around other like-minded optimists—people who saw the glass half full—or maybe all the way full, and not half empty.

The day was outstanding! There was so much energy, passion, and positivity in the room. I knew I was with "my people." Since getting involved with the Optimist Club, I've seen outstanding leadership and cutting-edge speakers as well as meeting optimistic people who want to make a difference in the world. The experience fills my heart and mind at every meeting I attend.

Research conducted by Martin Seligman, a leader within the field of Positive Psychology and professor at the University of Pennsylvania, suggested that leaders, entrepreneurs, and athletes who practice optimism are more likely to experience:

- A longer life. Optimists live longer than pessimists. They experience fewer infectious diseases, are less likely to have cancer, and have overall better health habits than pessimists.

- Better performance, consistently. Optimists perform better under pressure and have more consistent results than pessimists.
- Less stress, and more self-confidence and resilience. Optimism decreases the bad and increases the good.

I don't know about you, but I want to experience all of these benefits! The point is, you can. You have a choice.

Martin Seligman's work on "explanatory style" gives us powerful insight on this topic of optimism. Seligman argues that our explanatory style determines whether we are an optimist or pessimist. Our explanatory style is how we explain to ourselves why we experience a particular event as being either positive or negative. For example, an optimist believes that successes and positive events will continue and are not a fluke. An optimist also believes that they are the cause of good events in their lives; that good events don't just happen because of luck or things outside of their control.

Over time, we've all developed an explanatory style based on our experiences and on the experiences of those around us. But we can change our explanatory style by shifting how we explain events in our lives. We can change how we see events in our life—such as difficulties, obstacles, and setbacks—and in turn, we can maintain our optimism and confidence.

One of the strategies I share in my book titled *Beyond Grit: Ten Powerful Practices to Gain the High-Performing Edge* is a strategy I call Three OPP Strategy. When presented with a difficulty, you identify three opportunities. Instead of dwelling on the negative, taking the issue personally, or believing that bad events will continue, you choose to see the silver lining.

We all experience challenging situations. In fact, obstacles and setbacks are a given. It's how we respond to them that matters.

How would your life change if you worked to always see

failures and obstacles as opportunities? Think about it by using the Three OPP Strategy.

- First, think of a difficulty you are experiencing right now. Maybe your company is not positioned to meet its financial goals this year or your kid is misbehaving at home.
- Second, consider at least three opportunities that come from this difficulty. Perhaps this difficulty provides an opportunity for you to reexamine your goals, to spend more time with your child, or to simply focus on the things that are going well instead of dwelling on the things that aren't.

When you decide to choose optimism, you are more creative and excited about the possibilities. You have an energized perspective on what you are experiencing right now instead of dwelling in anxiety or focusing on worst-case scenarios.

Choosing optimism helps you expect that something good will come from everything. Choosing optimism helps you begin to see challenges as leading you to something better.

I know you are going to love this book by the Roseville Area Optimist Club. It is full of stories and inspiration to help you choose optimism. If you keep choosing optimism—and if you never stop believing that good events will continue as well as searching for the possibilities for you, your family, and your team—you'll take off beyond boundaries! And *Voices of Optimism* will help you do so.

With optimism,

Cindra Kamphoff, Ph.D., CMPC, CEO Mentally Strong Consulting, professional speaker, and coach.

Author, *Beyond Grit: Ten Powerful Practices to Gain the High-Performing Edge*

More at: CindraKamphoff.com or BeyondGrit.comw

Preface

This book began with a man and a book.

A few years ago I met Don Salverda, founder and president of the Roseville Area Optimist Club, for coffee. Following our meeting, Don mailed to me a copy of Hal Urban's book *Life's Greatest Lessons*. Instead of letting the book ripen on my bedside table, I began to read it and continued to read a chapter each morning.

At around the same time, I was referring a neighborhood young person for lawn-mowing jobs. I also loaned Hal Urban's book to James. The night before James returned to his junior year at Wheaton College in Wheaton, Illinois, he finished reading the book and wrote the thank-you note that is reproduced on pages xix and xx. With permission from James, I forwarded a copy of his note to Don, who was pleased and impressed.

During the summer of 2017, I invited James to attend an Optimist Club meeting and to meet Don. As James and I carpooled, we talked about work. I started to think about things I could tell him to prevent his learning some of life's lessons "the hard way"—as I'd learned them.

Fortunately, I caught myself before I dumped on James a mound of questionable advice. I asked myself, "Who am I to be giving James—or anyone!—advice?" But it occurred to me that I belong to an organization—our club—whose members are civic leaders, elected officials, and accomplished business people. They are dedicated to the tenets of Optimism International—the development of youth, their community, and themselves. *They* are the people whose advice would be worth having.

By listening to the introductions of members and guests during our lunch meetings, I knew that members of our club had more than one valuable story to share with an eager young person. I submitted a proposal for this book to Don and the board of directors. With important input from them, the project was approved.

We invited members and guest speakers to contribute a story from their life experiences to be included in this book. We anticipated the stories would be interesting and worth reading, but we vastly underestimated the blazing original-ity—and unabashed candor and sincerity—with which the authors expressed themselves.

We now invite you to savor our stories, enjoy them, and share them—along with your own story—with someone who is important to you.

Sue Filbin, editor and designer
Member, Roseville Area Optimist Club
Roseville, Minnesota
July 2018

August 14, 2016

Hi Sue,

My plan to read one chapter of Hal Urban's book every day fell apart, and I ended up reading about 85% of the book last night. But alas, I finished it.

This was the first time I had come in contact with Urban's writing, and it was also the first self-help/development book that I have dived into. Both offered new and insightful ideas. I really liked how everything Hal said was packaged. None of the concepts were necessarily groundbreaking or new, but they were explained in such a way that I felt like I had missed something that had been hiding in plain sight my whole life.

One of my favorite take-aways was that of goals vs. dreams. I love the idea that a goal is a dream with a deadline. Urban's strategy of making a to-do list and then looking at it often really resonated with me. I also appreciated how Hal would revise his goals, and would adjust them accordingly. I have a hard time giving a goal up once I set it. Hal showed me that it was OK to change priorities and therefore change goals.

He also spoke about how we are free to do anything we want—so I have no excuse to keep goals that are unnecessary. I can choose to let them go. I also really liked Urban's chapter about having fun and laughing. It really does do a great deal of good and I will be working on practicing "fun" as I go back to college. Many thanks for lending me the book, Sue. I do very much appreciate it.

With cheer,

James Sorensen

Hi Sue,   8-14-16

My plan to read one chapter of Hal Urban's book every day fell apart, and I ended up reading about 85% of the book last night. But alas, I finished it. This was the first time I had come in contact with Urban's writing, and it was also the first self-help/development book that I have dove into. Both offered new and insightful ideas. I really liked how everything Hal said was packaged. None of the concepts were necessarily groundbreaking or new, but they were explained in such a way that I felt like I had missed something that had been hiding in plain sight my whole life. One of my favorite take-aways was that of goals vs. dreams. I love the idea that a goal is a dream with a deadline. Urban's strategy of making a to-do list and then looking at it often really resonated with me. I also appreciated how Hal would revise his goals, and would adjust them accordingly. I have a hard time giving a goal up once I set it. Hal showed me that it was ok to change priorities and therefore change goals. He also spoke about how we are free to do anything we want. So I have no excuse to keep goals that are unnecessary. I can choose to let them go. I also really liked Urban's chapter about having fun and laughing. It really does do a great deal of good and I will be working on practicing "fun" as I go back to college. Many thanks for lending me the book Sue, I do very much appreciate it.   With cheer, James Svensen

Introduction

From my experiences as a consultant and elected official in private and public entities, I believe that most people aspire to do what's right—for the greater good, themselves, and their communities. But during the time of the 2016 presidential election as well as today, there is too much cynicism, negativity, frustration, and despair with too many people.

As a very positive person, ready to "do somethng" to foster increased positivity with friends, clients, and the community, I was aware of the Optimist organization, having seen the Optimist International (O.I.) booth at the Minnesota State Fair for many years, but I'd never taken action.

In 2016 I stopped at their booth and left my name and phone number. I soon received a call from Terry Gorman, governor of our region within O.I. (Dakotas-Manitoba-Minnesota). Terry and I met for coffee along with Barb Einan, a friend and longtime Roseville resident, to learn about the Optimist organization and to express our interest in forming a new club.

The three of us agreed to meet again and to include a core group of local leaders, colleagues from the Roseville Rotary Club, and friends from other associations. Interest among those of us attending the meeting was strong. We agreed to establish a new Optimist club—the 23rd in the state of Minnesota.

Two informational meetings were held to further promote the idea of the club and to expand our group. Our first official meeting was held on January 13, 2017. We met over a buffet lunch at the Radisson Hotel in Roseville. Table hosts distributed information to guests. Our first speaker was Scott Welle, a high-energy speaker whose theme was "Outperform the Norm." We started our new group with 29 charter members. Subsequently a board of directors was named.

Seventeen months after our club was founded, we welcomed our 100th member. We've learned that people are eager to associate with positive people, hear inspiring speakers, and participate in fulfilling activities and projects within the community.

This book is the embodiment of the positive, generous perspective of our members and speakers. Many responded to our invitation to provide a story from their life experiences that a young person would find to be valuable. Some stories relate to the influence of family and memories from the author's youth. Others mention their current family, historical events, or work-related lessons. You will identify with some and learn from others. Our goal is that your own outlook becomes more positive by reflecting on our "Voices of Optimism."

In optimism,
Don Salverda, founder and charter president
Roseville Area Optimist Club
Roseville, Minnesota

Optimist International

Mission
By providing hope and positive vision, Optimists bring out the best in youth, our communities, and ourselves.

Vision
Optimist International will be recognized worldwide as the premier volunteer organization that values all children and helps them develop to their full potential.

Purposes
- To develop optimism as a philosophy of life utilizing the tenets of the Optimist Creed
- To promote an active interest in good government and civic affairs
- To inspire respect for the law
- To promote patriotism and work for international accord and friendship among all people
- To aid and encourage the development of youth in the belief that the giving of one's self in service to others will advance the well-being of humankind, community life, and the world.

Optimist Creed

Promise yourself

To be so strong that nothing can disturb your peace of mind.

To talk health, happiness, and prosperity to every person you meet.

To make all your friends feel that there is something in them.

To look at the sunny side of everything and make your optimism come true.

To think only of the best, to work only for the best, and to expect only the best.

To be just as enthusiastic about the success of others as you are about your own.

To forget the mistakes of the past and press on to the greater achievements of the future.

To wear a cheerful countenance at all times and give every living creature you meet a smile.

To give so much time to the improvement of yourself that you have no time to criticize others.

To be too large for worry, too noble for anger, too strong for fear, and too happy to permit the presence of trouble.

Charter Members

Patrick Antonen
Dave Bartholomay
Zola Burns*
Bill Dircks
Barbara Einan
Michael Ericson
Allen Gerdin
Terry Gorman*
Lou Hastert
Gary Havir
Jon Heyer
Craig Johnson
Jamey Johnson
Chuck Kadrie
Kevin Keenan*

Darrel LeBarron
Stephen Manweiler
Mary Jo McGuire*
Lynne Megan*
Don Salverda*
David Schaps*
Karen Schaub*
Mark E. Smith
Curt Stockford
Patrick Trudgeon*
Liz Uram
Craig Waldron*
Julie Wearn
Andy Wells
*Board member

Board Members

All that we behold is full of blessings.
WILLIAM WORDSWORTH

Board Members

Don Salverda, President
Terry Gorman, Vice President
Zola Burns, Treasurer
David Schaps, Secretary
Kevin Keenan, Director
Mary Jo McGuire, Director
Lynne Megan, Director
Karen Schaub, Director
Patrick Trudgeon, Director
Craig Waldron, Director

Thoughts on Leadership, Service, Happiness, and Fulfillment

Don Salverda, President of
the Roseville Area Optimist Club

I'm excited about our newly formed Optimist Club in the Roseville and surrounding areas. I believe strongly in our mission and purpose. I'm equally excited about sharing a few thoughts about the importance of attitudes, taking action, and continuing lifelong learning as they relate to leadership, service, happiness, and fulfillment.

Experience-wise, I've carved out a very satisfying career. After a brief start in engineering and sales, I eventually began a career focused on leadership development and government service. I have been fortunate to have served in a number of leadership roles in the private sector, the public sector as an elected official, and in several community and professional organizations.

The most important life lessons I've learned in over 50 years, and the advice I share with others, are:

1. The importance of having a positive attitude and mindset

A positive attitude sparks desire, which is key to effectiveness, success, and fulfillment. Many noted authorities have spoken on the power of attitude.

"As a man thinketh, so is he."—James Allen, author of *As a Man Thinketh*

"Your attitude is like the engine that drives your car." —Jim Rohn, author of *The Five Major Pieces of the Life Puzzle*

"Attitude is a choice—the most important one you'll ever make."—Hal Urban, author of *Life's Greatest Lessons*

"A simple belief about ourselves guides a large part of our lives."—Carol Dweck, Ph.D., author of *Mindset: The New Psychology of Success*

Much of the news we experience on television and in print is filled with negativism. We need to guard our minds with what we think about. Jim Rohn had a great quote, "Nourish the mind like you would your body. The mind cannot survive on junk food."

We need to be optimists and be positive thinkers.

---

2. The importance of being proactive

People seem to fall into three categories:
- Those who make things happen
- Those who watch things happen
- Those who are oblivious of things that are happening

Nothing happens without positive action. Ideas are a dime a dozen. Thoughts without action are empty promises. It's easy to be paralyzed with analysis and indecision. I believe strongly in the quote, "If it's to be, it's up to me."

We need to be proactive and take positive action.

---

3. The importance of lifelong learning

Dr. Stephen Covey, the highly influential author of *The 7 Habits of Highly Effective People*, said that highly effective people continually "sharpen their saw."

I believe our ultimate responsibility is to invest in our own development. Yet I find too many individuals who believe they have little, if any, responsibility for their own development. They have little interest in growing and investing in themselves. I believe we separate ourselves from the crowd by where we invest our time and dollars.

We need to be lifelong learners.

In summary, I believe that effectiveness, success, happiness, and fulfillment are the result of having a positive attitude, taking positive action, and being committed to continuous learning and self-development. I further believe that if we adopt these three lessons, we will demonstrate needed leadership in our undertakings and spheres of influence, and will inspire others by our example.

As Denny Sanford—entrepreneur, philanthropist, high school friend, and classmate—says, "We need to aspire to inspire before we expire."

Don Salverda

Education: B.M.E., mechanical engineering (industrial engineering specialty), University of Minnesota

Work: Leadership and management consultant, elected Ramsey County Commissioner for 18 years, and held leadership roles in a number of professional and volunteer organizations including the Association of Minnesota Counties, Ramsey County League of Local Governments, Sales and Marketing Executives of Minneapolis, Roseville Chamber of Commerce, Roseville and Minnesota Jaycees, and the Roseville Rotary Club.

Book: *Life's Greatest Lessons* by Hal Urban

Quote: Words are the arsenal of leadership. —Winston Churchill

Don Salverda at Office Depot, making handouts for our Optimist Club meeting.

To Young Adults

Terry K. Gorman, Vice President

I would like to suggest or recommend some life lessons for you to take action on earlier in your career as you travel your path of life, and interact with your community and develop your career.

1. Take care of yourself—body, mind and soul.

Develop and maintain an optimistic and positive attitude. To that end, hang out and associate with positive-minded friends and colleagues. Every day, try to eat a healthy breakfast and regular meals. Be aware of your daily calorie intake and adjust your diet as needed to maintain a healthy weight.

Work out for 30 minutes three or four times a week. It can be as simple as a brisk walk. Keep mentally sharp and challenge your brain every day. Read, do crossword puzzles and so forth. Schedule regular medical checkups and exams. Be mindful that overdoing or overdosing on anything can and will be harmful to your health and wellness.

Take your vacation days to rest up, revitalize and renew. Don't turn them down or turn them back in.

2. Develop and cultivate friends and friendships.

There may be times when a problem(s) may seem

insurmountable. Ask for help, don't give up and talk to your doctor, minister, counselor or a friend about the problem or issue.

3. Get to know your neighbors and make friends.

Listen to the news. Know what is happening and is important in your community, your state and with national issues. Be informed on political issues and make time to vote in every election. Volunteer in your community to help others less fortunate. If you see or hear something that does not seem right, say something to a local official.

4. Education is the key to your success.

Never stop learning. Take classes outside of your major interest areas or take classes just for fun. Find a career or job that is meaningful and fun to do every day. If your job gets old or boring, try to move up or prepare yourself to move on. Set your goals high and adjust them as you make progress.

5. Money.

Develop a budget and work to stick to it. Open a savings account, contribute to it regularly and have six to 12 months of savings to cover expenses. With your first and every job, start and continue to contribute to your retirement savings plan/account. Get professional help in managing your monies. Make your monies work harder than you do.

6. Start a tradition.

Invite friends and family to be part of your tradition. As time passes, you may want to develop additional traditions.

7. Be courteous.

Develop an attitude of politeness, be civil and do unto others as you would want them to do unto you.

8. Hiring experts.

If you're not handy or able to make simple repairs, use the internet for assistance. Find a reliable, trustworthy and cost-effective mechanic, plumber, electrician, and general repair person. Know your limitations and when it's time to hire a professional.

9. Social media.

Be cautious about what you post on social media. The content can be out there forever. Take time and think before you post something. As I once heard, and I believe to be sound advice: Do not post anything online or write in an email anything that you would not want to have read out loud in a court of law or for your grandmother to hear. Social media can easily be overdone and can lead to relationship- and career-ending issues. Remember that much of the information posted on social media is not accurate or true, so cross-check facts and information with other reliable sources.

10. Life is not always fair.

Be ready for the unexpected and ready to take advantage of opportunities.

Terry K. Gorman

Education: B.A., industrial education K-12; M.S., comprehensive industrial education K-12; M.S., industrial processes and safety engineering, University of Wisconsin-Platteville

Work: Retired from the U.S. Navy— 33 years; teaching high school; and working as the Director of Environmental Health, Safety, and Security at Macalester College, 38 years. Member of Optimist International since 1974; Distinguished District Governor, Optimist International, 2016-2017.

Book: *D-Day June 6, 1944: The Climactic Battle of World War II* by Stephen E. Ambrose

Quote: If you see something, say something. —National motto since September 12, 2001

More: https://www.linkedin.com/in/terry-k-gorman-a2b80311/

Painful Blessings

Zola Burns, Treasurer

"Easy Does It." "One Day at a Time." "Let Go and Let God." "Pass It On." "If It's to Be, It's Up to Me."

My heart is full of gratitude to those who helped me learn to embrace and live by these short, simple phrases. I didn't realize I was searching for these tools, but when I discovered them, I knew I needed them. They support my optimistic outlook on life.

I am the oldest of four siblings—two girls and two boys. As a child, I had everything I needed—food, clothing, a bedroom shared with my sister, and my siblings as playmates. I had everything I could want, too—Barbie dolls, a playhouse in the backyard, a purple Schwinn bicycle, skates, swimming lessons, and family pets named McKnight, Midnight, and Sonny. Our pets were strays that my dad would rescue from a job site or the side of a highway or on a sidewalk somewhere. He'd bring them home for us to play with and love. My childhood was full of expectation, hope, and optimism about the future.

I loved my school experience from elementary to high school. I never missed one single day, and I felt sad if school was closed due to winter snowfall. I was a tutor for special ed students. I worked in the office and did a variety of assignments to help out the school secretaries and teachers. I volunteered to repair and even design costumes for the drama club. I was in the presence of teachers and staff who were warm and kind, appreciative, and optimistic. I respected and admired the demeanor and behavior of these adults as much as their knowledge. My personal optimism flourished during my high school years.

As a teenager, I wasn't popular or out-going. I wasn't athletic and I didn't participate in any team sports like volleyball, track, or gymnastics. I never had a boyfriend or attended a school dance or prom. On occasion, I felt a bit like an "odd man out," but mostly it didn't matter too much to me that I wasn't cool. My mom was very talented at creative arts such as embroidery, crocheting, knitting, sewing, and crafts, and she enjoyed teaching all these skills to me. Many of the projects I completed during this stage of my life are still on display in the homes of my family members. To this day I feel immense joy in creating gifts of my own handiwork. My self-confidence grew, as did my ability to plan, budget, troubleshoot, and apply the self-discipline to complete what I had started. I strived for perfection and was never satisfied with simply good enough. I felt optimistic that my talents would somehow be put to good use in my future.

My dad valued work. He worked 24/7. A plaque hung in my dad's office that read, "Home is Where You Go When You're Tired of Being Nice to People," and he proved that to be true time and time again. My siblings and I never risked inviting a friend over for dinner or to sleep over. We couldn't predict when our dad would get home, how intoxicated he'd be, or if he'd want to pick a fight. This became the elephant in the room in our home. This was a sad reality, but thanks to courage, hope, optimism, and the grace of God, that was only part of our family's story, and not the entire story.

I was 17 years old the day I graduated from high school. My first and most important goal was to leave home. The day after my graduation, I packed up and never looked back. As I write this, I'm astonished that I never spent another night in my parents' home after that day.

My dad had helped me get a job as a housekeeper for a wealthy lady which I did for four years during high school. She wrote a strong letter of recommendation for me that convinced the owner of a resort in northern Minnesota that I was capable of being a reliable summer-season cabin maid. I worked hard, had a blast with my new friends and new freedom, and ended the season with a check for $300. Tips were everything even back then.

At the end of the season, I found a roommate, a cheap apartment, and a second-shift job at a factory where I was responsible for pumping out 8,000 tubes of split-shot sinkers per shift. I may have been very naïve, but my positive attitude and optimism made me feel as if I was on top of the world.

I had no college plans or aspirations. Higher education wasn't a family value, so I decided to go to vocational school because it was free for students under age 21 at that time. I enrolled in the cosmetology program. My classmates, teachers, and models made the program great fun. I graduated, took my board exam for a license, and worked as a hair stylist for three long years. The biggest surprise about cosmetology school was it is where I met my life-long best friend, Lynette. This is when I accepted with certainty that people come into our lives at special times for special reasons. Over time, we revealed to one another the similarities we shared from our childhood families and the role alcoholism had played in our family experiences. What a truly amazing realization and relief to no longer feel isolated by that secret.

My new friend's family was further into recovery than my family was. They invited me to travel with them to Denver to attend the 45th International Alcoholics Anonymous Conference. I didn't know what to expect, but I was excited to go. I couldn't have imagined how important this one event would be to the rest of my life. Attendees echoed the phrases you read at the beginning of my story as warm friendly greetings to old friends and new friends alike. Recovery is a painful blessing, and a connection like no other I know. The love, hope, and optimism that is present and shared makes your heart burst with gratitude.

My dad entered treatment three different times before he surrendered and started his recovery. His daily efforts and life-long devotion to his recovery (including a couple of brief relapses) give me strong reason to be optimistic that any person can overcome whatever challenges he or she may face.

Looking back, I can see clearly that both of my parents had hearts of gold and an enormously optimistic spirit that they instilled in me. Thanks to recovery and the gifts of AA, our family came to be courageous, accepting, forgiving, and happy. We are a family of rejoicing eternal optimists.

I have many favorite quotes but my most favorite is, "Gratitude is not only the greatest of all virtues, but the parent of all the others." *Marcus Tullius Cicero*. This is taped to the inside of my bathroom vanity door where I read it every morning and every evening to remind myself of the many blessings in my life.

My greatest blessings are my parents, my siblings, my husband, and my life-long best friend Lynette. Other cherished and treasured blessings in my life include more family, friends, my health, and my work. My actions and choices have made me a very lucky woman. And through everything, I remain grateful and optimistic that "The Best is Yet to Come."

Zola Burns

Education: Associate of Arts, legal administrative assistant, Century College, White Bear Lake, Minnesota

Work: Since 1989, administration manager, Gausman & Moore Associates, Inc., mechanical and electrical consulting engineers.

Book: *An Enemy Called Average* by John L. Mason

Quote: Gratitude is not only the greatest of all virtues, but the parent of all the others. —Marcus Tullius Cicero

Zola Burns with her siblings, left to right: John, Adam, Susie, and Zola.

You Are the Best! Act Like It!

David R. Schaps, Secretary

I grew up in Litchfield, Minnesota, a city of about 7,000 people located ninety minutes west of the Twin Cities. Our high school was not that big, averaging 450-500 kids in grades 9-12. But our marching band was big. We had three grades in the band, and we always had a band of 170-200 of us out on the streets. And it was a great band—the Litchfield Marching Dragons. We won award after award in marching band parades, year after year. We competed with the big suburban schools that had more kids, more funding, and more opportunities. We were known as a great and very competitive marching band.

Marching band practice started at 6 a.m. the Monday after school got out for the summer; 6 a.m. to noon. Then most kids were off to summer jobs. For two weeks, we would assemble our nearly 200 kids and march up and down 10th Street, which runs from the Litchfield Civic Arena, past the high school, and down to Litchfield's main street, which is Sibley Avenue. The street also basically forms the northern border of the town.

You were never late to practice in the morning—or you were doing push-ups! I was proud to play three years in that band carrying a brass sousaphone (1st chair senior year!). We did not go to expensive band camps or hold additional band practices other than regular music class during the school year. We had two weeks of early-morning intense practice and then we were supposed to start competing and beat the "big" schools all over the state in local parade competitions and city festivals.

Everyone in town woke up to the marching band playing our traditional song at 6 a.m. because the city is small enough that the sound of the band practicing travels across the whole community. Litchfield also has a distinctive drum cadence that has been played year after year, so the entire community knows the band is coming down the street upon hearing just a few bars of that beat.

Dave Schaps, marching with his sousaphone in the 2016 Litchfield Alumni Marching Band.

Our band director was Mr. Keith Johnson. He was, and is still an unbelievable ball of positive, forward-moving energy. His wit is sharp as a tack. He's actually the mayor of Litchfield now after retiring from teaching music at the high school for over thirty years. Mr. Johnson is always cracking a joke, flashing a smile, and asking you how you are doing. His positivity is infectious. But he was also unbelievably focused in leading the band. You showed up on time. Your phasing in your marching and foot-fall was exactly precise. You did not get out of step. You hit every note with perfection. You stuck that final note with gusto! And if you didn't, Mr. Johnson never singled you out, yelled at you, or belittled you. His leading and coaching style was not one seeking to find fault. He never threatened to cut anyone from the marching band. He'd call out, *"C'mon, Folks"* in his booming, band-teacher voice, *"You're the best out there! Act like it!!!"* And then back and forth along 10th Street we would go. Over and over again. Consequently, it is common knowledge in Litchfield to never drive down 10th Street in June because you ran into the band—and the band wasn't going to move—your car was.

Taking those experiences with me on this amazing journey called life—from being a high-school kid from a small town, fast forwarding to adulthood with a wife, home, and two wonderful children who are, as of this writing, ages 3 and 5—has always helped me during tough experiences. Whether it be the tests in college and law school, dealing with difficult situations and issues at work, and now learning to be the best father I can be, I feel prepared.

In addition, I am technically on my second career path after switching from over nine years in the city-management field to establishing a rewarding new municipal-, labor-, and employment-law practice providing city-attorney services at Barna, Guzy & Steffen, a mid-sized Twin Cities suburban law firm. That was a huge change from leaving a profession in which I was well versed and would have enjoyed until retirement.

But during that journey, there have been many times when I have felt that I was grossly underqualified at tackling a significant new issue, problem, challenge, or case. Sometimes you just don't know what you don't know. In addition, when I did take on that huge new challenge, the reward for success was usually not huge financial gains or awards. It was usually an even larger challenge. But when those times happen, I remember Mr. Johnson shouting at the band at the top of his lungs that, *"You're the best! Act like it!!!"*

Don't shy away from tough challenges; seek them out. Actually seeing the right result come from hard work is immeasurably satisfying. As Teddy Roosevelt said, "There is no greater joy in the world than the opportunity to work hard at work worth doing." Talk to people. Ask questions. Always act with kindness. And always remember: *You're the best out there! Act like it!*

David R. Schaps

Education: B.A., political science, Gustavus Adolphus College; M.A., public administration, Hamline University; J.D., Hamline University School of Law

Work: Since 2014, associate attorney, Barna, Guzy & Steffen; three years as assistant city administrator, City of Oakdale; five years as assistant to the city administrator, City of Oakdale; a year-and-a-half as administrative intern with City of Oakdale; sergeant level one, Minnesota House of Representatives, attached to the local government committee for the 2005 session.

Book: *Positive Words, Powerful Results* by Hal Urban

Quote: Real difficulties can be overcome; it is only the imaginary ones that are unconquerable. —Theodore N. Vail

More: www.linkedin.com/in/dave-schaps-ba4a30b

Don't Look at Yourself as a Victim

Kevin Keenan

The easy way out when something goes wrong is to picture yourself as a victim. That way you are never responsible for what happens to you. It happened because of something else or someone else, but not you.

A personal experience demonstrates this. At the age of 46, I was a lawyer with a great firm in downtown Minneapolis. I had a great wife, three terrific teenage kids and a very nice house in one of the suburbs. Life was good. Then I had a stroke.

I was lucky to live. The brain surgeon said I had only twenty minutes to live. Most people who have the type of stroke I had die, and most of those who survive end up in a nursing home. I was fortunate, but I didn't feel fortunate. I felt as if my life was over even though I was still alive. I eventually had brain surgery and then extensive rehabilitation. I was in the hospital nearly three months.

During my hospital stay, I was in bed and realized that my career as a lawyer was probably over. (I tried to go back, but I did not have the mental stamina to continue as a trial lawyer). My dad was with me in the hospital room. My dad had many terrible things happen to him, but he was the most optimistic person I have ever known. I asked my dad how he stayed so optimistic with all the terrible things that happened to him. He said: "Kevin, self pity is like peeing in your pants. It's a nice warm feeling **at first**."

That is what I needed to hear. I was feeling sorry for myself. I was looking at myself as a victim of bad luck. I promised myself that I would not become a victim. I was going to take responsibility for my actions and not blame bad luck.

As mentioned above, I tried to go back to work, but eventually retired at the age of 48. I didn't let myself become a victim. Since I retired, I have been president of the Ramsey County School Safety Patrol Foundation, president of the Northwest Suburban Gavel Club, president of my local Rotary Club, treasurer of my church's Knights of Columbus council and vice-president of the Consumer Advisory Council of the USPS.

My Advice: Don't view yourself as a victim; take responsibility for your actions. Don't blame others or events for what happens to you and remain optimistic, no matter what.

Kevin Keenan

Education: B.A., economics, St. Mary's University, Winona, MN; J.D., University of Minnesota

Work: Bassford Remele, P.A.

Book: I enjoy any book written by John Sanford.

Quote: Do your best, prepare for the worst—but accept what God gives you. —Anonymous

Growing Up Positive

Mary Jo McGuire

My story is dedicated to my mother, Mary Elaine McGuire, a positive role model, inspiration and the most optimistic person I know.

"If you think you're beaten, you are.
If you think you dare not, you don't.
If you'd like to win, but you think you can't,
It's almost a cinch you won't.

"You've got to think high to rise,
You've got to believe in yourself
Ere you can win the prize.
For it's not always the stronger and swifter one who wins,
But the one who thinks she can."
Paraphrased from a poem by Walter Wintle.

I grew up with this saying from my mother and my grand-mother. We were a household of six kids and a mother and father where positivity and a positive attitude were the norm. How lucky we were! Mom would always say, "If you can't say something nice about someone, don't say anything at all." And if we did say something negative about someone, we had to follow up with three positives about them!

To this day, we also play a game called, "Who is the greatest?" It usually starts with someone feeling sad. If it was my brother, John, someone would burst out with, "Who is the greatest John in the world?" and we would all shout together, "Our John," and then we would proceed to go through the entire group of siblings and friends gathered, with, "Who is the greatest _____(Mike, Mary Jo, Jeanne, Mark, Jeff, Mom, Dad) in the world?" followed by: "Our ____(Mike, Mary Jo, Jeanne, Mark, Jeff, Mom, Dad). We would all tingle in anticipation, waiting for our turn, and it was amazing how much better you felt when you had the affirmation of the group.

Yes, we did grow up in a very affirming household and I am the better for it. One might wonder if I ever have doubts or if I ever feel bad or negative. Well, the answer is, "I try not to," but it does happen, and then I do try to talk myself out of it. As Mother would say, "You are sad, if you say/think you are sad." I would argue, but came to realize that I did have the power in my mind to control my thoughts. Having a positive attitude will bring about many more positive things in our lives.

When my father died suddenly at age 58, it was difficult to think positive. When Mom commented, "The one good thing...," her friend stopped her and said, "Mary, there's *no* good thing." Mom continued, "The one good thing was that he did not suffer." And that was true. We all survived with the very well-known and powerful Serenity Prayer: "God grant me the serenity to accept what I cannot change, the courage to change the things I can, and the wisdom to know the difference." It does make a difference.

Adjusting to my father's untimely death took a lot out of all of us. I took advantage of this opportunity to make some changes in my own life. I quit my job (which I had been wanting to do), moved home and went to law school. This change in my life set a number of things in motion that were transformational. It was a positive attitude and a spirit of optimism that drove my next crucial life decisions.

I had been deeply involved in student government in both college and law school, and wanted to work in the area of public policy. I had no idea how it would happen or that the opportunity to do so would present itself in a very unexpected way. I had graduated from law school and was studying for the bar exam when I received a phone call asking me to be the candidate for state representative in my legislative district. I was surprised, intrigued, and a bit nervous.

It had been difficult for the party to find someone to run against a popular fourteen-year incumbent. Some party activists had seen me at my precinct caucus and thought I might be a good candidate because I had a lot of positive energy. As a first-time candidate challenging an incumbent, my chances of winning were slim. The filing deadline was the next day, so I thought about it overnight, and gratefully had the confidence and optimism to say yes!

I filed for office ahead of the 4:30 p.m. deadline and found out later that evening that at 3:30 p.m. that afternoon, my fifty-three-year-old opponent had died of complications from an appendicitis attack. I was the only one who had filed in my own party, so ended up running against his campaign manager who had become the candidate in his party to fill the vacancy. It was one of the top-ten contested legislative races in the state, and it took a lot of hard work.

I won that election and was a member of the Minnesota House of Representatives for the next fourteen years. I was excited to be working in a field in which I could have a positive impact on people's lives. I then became a victim of a court redistricting plan, causing me to leave my position earlier than expected. The spirit of optimism held when, with the closing of one door, another one opened. My departure from the House of Representatives led me to a fulfilling eight years of working in legislative advocacy and civic education. At this point, a senate seat opened and I won that seat in a special election. After serving two years in the senate, I was once again a victim of court redistricting and once again found another open door. This time, it led me to the perfect fit in my current position as a Ramsey County Commissioner. What a great thing!

I make a game of being positive. I call it the "Opposite Game" or "Switch." When something negative or unwanted happens, or if things are not going as you would like, you force yourself to think and say the opposite, the positive. You call "Switch" and get your brain to "switch" from a negative thought to a positive one. It is useful in major and minor circumstances.

Recently, I had a flight cancel due to bad weather. The frustration of spending the entire next day flying standby gave me the opportunity to play the game. I forced myself to think the opposite of what I was thinking. Instead of thinking about how upset I was to be "wasting" time at the airport, I turned it around to tell myself how "fortunate" I was to have time to myself, to get work done, to get exercise walking the concourse, to find the positive in a negative situation. My attitude was crucial in helping me to accept the circumstances over which I had no control and make the best of them.

I credit my early foundation of trying to make the best of tough situations that are not in my control with helping me thrive through these major life transitions. Admittedly, they haven't all been as easy as one might like, but they have helped make me who I am today. And I am able to work in a field in which I have the opportunity to make a positive difference in people's lives.

I am grateful to the Roseville Area Optimist Club for reinforcing how important it is to think positively, be optimistic, turn negatives into positives and make the best of every situation. It is something I intend to do for the rest of my life.

Mary Jo McGuire

Education: B.A., business administration, St. Catherine University; M.A., public administration, Harvard University Kennedy School of Government; J.D., Hamline University School of Law

Work: Ramsey County Commissioner, District 2, since 2012; adjunct professor in the Masters of Organizational Leadership (MAOL) Department, St. Catherine University; State Senator, Minnesota Senate, 2010-2012; State Representative, Minnesota House of Representatives, 1989-2002; adjunct professor, Hamline University; guest lecturer at West Point Military Academy.

Book: *The Four Agreements* by Don Miguel Ruiz

Quote: S(he) has achieved success who has lived well, laughed often, and loved much. —Bessie Anderson Stanley

My Mother's Plan for a Good Life

Lynne Megan

I learned early in my life that one must accept the life that is before us and the challenges that we are faced with, and move forward positively! I grew up number eight of nine children in a small town in northwest Iowa. My daddy died when I was 12. My parents both had only an eighth-grade education. When my daddy died, my mother was 51 years old. Instead of accepting a life of poverty, my mom stood tall (she never made it over five feet tall, though) and made a plan for her life—our family's life.

Mother studied for and took her GED within six months of my daddy passing. She then applied for nursing school, was accepted, and enrolled within a year of her dear husband's death. For two years, she drove 40 miles each way to Sioux Falls, SD, to Sioux Valley School of Nursing. Mother was 52 years old; her classmates were 18, 19, and 20 years old! Her classmates voted her most likable, primarily because of her positive, can-do attitude. She graduated in the top of her class.

One of mother's favorite motivators during her education trek was when my dear friend, Randy—while we were playing in the neighborhood—would open our back door and yell in to Mother, "Are you a doctor yet?" This gave Mother the courage and fortitude to push forward and study harder.

As I write this, I still get chills from that question Randy so innocently asked! I have told him in recent years when I see him while visiting my hometown how he impacted my mother. He is always humbled when I share the memory with him. Now, this memorable experience is coming from the "class clown" and the one *always* in trouble in class! Who knew his message would be so encouraging and impactful!

Mother's career as a nurse began at age 53. Now, needless to say, upon her beginning her illustrious career late in life, life continued to bring challenges with her large family. We had four family members in Viet Nam. All came home with no physical injury. At age 23, my brother—child number six—died unexpectedly on a hiking trip on an Alaskan glacier. His body was not found for a year and a half after he went missing. Through this tough, tough time, Mother remained positive that we would find Randy and we would celebrate his life. Upon receiving his life insurance benefit from the U.S. Army, Mother purchased a beautiful piano. She dearly loved playing her beloved piano and felt close to her dear son while playing. Mind you, this woman was a self-taught pianist, and she played wonderfully!

Mother continued her career as a nurse until she was 67 years old, working at the local hospital and nursing homes. Upon her retirement, she became a counselor, working with individuals with disabilities. Together we learned to become passionate about our servant life.

I recall the story that Mother told one evening. While working at the nursing home, an elderly gentleman stood at the end of the hallway wanting Mother's attention. He yelled, "Waitress, waitress." This incensed Mother as she was so, so proud of her degree and her fortitude to become a nurse.

Mother lived a long and full life. In spite of her husband dying when they were both so young, she took on the role of single parenthood to the three of us at home. She persevered through the teenage years with us and supported us through our high school and college years. She loved travel and would travel the world following her children wherever they moved—across the U.S., Germany, Venezuela, and Japan. People in her small town would wonder where Alta got the money to travel and were openly jealous of her "vander lust." She lived in her own home until she was 91 and died happy at 94.5 years old. At her celebration of life, we "celebrated" this brave, strong, and beautiful woman.

My mother Alta's outlook on life and how she lived her life has guided and led me throughout my life. Always looking for the positive has been my lead. In my career, I am challenged daily to provide quality supports and services for individuals with disabilities, the most vulnerable of our citizens. Some days this is overwhelming. I sit back and muster up the courage and fortitude to go at it again and again.

My message to myself, my family, friends, and colleagues is to *always* take the time to learn, find time for fun, be true to yourself, treat others as you would treat yourself, and *love life*! Live life for today and not tomorrow!

Lynne Megan

Education: B.S., social work and psychology, Morningside College, Sioux City, Iowa; Mini MBAs from St. Thomas University, St. Paul, MN

Work: Since 2005, CEO of TSE, Inc., an employment and enrichment nonprofit supporting people with disabilities. Serves on many local, state, and national boards of directors.

Book: *A Higher Loyalty: Truth, Lies, and Leadership* by James Comey

Quote: Live life for today, not tomorrow. (This is my mantra.)

More: http://www.tse-inc.org/

Turn your face toward the sun
and the shadows fall behind you.
ANONYMOUS

How Are *You* … Today?

Karen Schaub

How are you? How many times in a day do we hear these words from someone we passed on the street, from a colleague, from a friend or from a sales associate? As psychologist David Caruso observes, "American culture demands that the answer to the question 'How are you?' is not just 'Good'…but we need to be 'Awesome.'"

And yes, some days I *am* awesome.

I question whether people really care how I am. This can seem like a huge question to answer on some days. I wonder: Do you mean right now? Do you mean how am I doing at work? Do you mean physically, how I am doing? Do you mean mentally how I am doing? Do you mean how am I doing with the loss of my father? What do you really mean? Does it matter to you how I answer the question, or do you just ask everyone you meet this question? If I tell you I am not fine, then what? Do you care to engage with me, if it might mean a heartfelt conversation? Or are you turned off if I tell you that I could not be better?

In the book *Option B* by Sheryl Sandberg, she suggests a different twist to the greeting, "How are you *today?*" This question seems to be more in the moment and it allows me a more optimistic answer, without thinking about everything in my life before I answer the question. I could respond, "I am great today, and I just came from an awesome Optimist Club meeting where we heard Senator Dave Durenberger who spoke about *Lessons Learned from Over 50 Years of Public, Private, Non-profit and Volunteer Sectors Leadership and Experiences.* And, how are you today?"

How can we take a simple question and answer it with heart, with focus and with optimism? I encourage all of us to think about how often we ask, "How are you today?" and about how often we really want a real answer and are willing to spend the time getting to know a person better.

Let's make it a habit to take time to ask the question, "How are you today?" and then listen openly to the answer, acknowledge the individual and respond in a way that is meaningful to you.

Karen Schaub

Education: B.A., community education, Minnesota State University, Mankato; M.A., education administration, University of St. Thomas

Work: Director of community education for Roseville Area School District, Minnesota.

Book: *Option B: Facing Adversity, Building Resilience, and Finding Joy* and *Lean In* by Sheryl Sandberg; *Originals* by Adam Grant

Quote: *Stepping Stones*

Isn't it strange that princes and kings
And clowns that appear in sawdust rings
And common folks like you and me
Are builders of community?

Each is given a bag of tools.
A block of clay and book of rules.
And each must make, ere life has flown.
A stumbling block or a stepping stone.

—Author unknown

Optimists are builders of stepping stones. If you want to get something done, who do you ask? You ask someone who has an optimistic personality; who understands how to do the right thing in the right way at the right time, even when no one is watching. These are important qualities in building a healthy community—whatever your description of community might be.

Optimism in Precarious Times

Pat Trudgeon

"I just want to do God's will. And He's allowed me to go up to the mountain. And I've looked over. And I've seen the Promised Land. I may not get there with you. But I want you to know tonight, that we, as a people, will get to the Promised Land." —*Rev. Dr. Martin Luther King Jr., the day before he was assassinated.*

As a student of history, I am always drawn to stories that take place in times of peril and upheaval. What especially makes these events remarkable is that when things look the bleakest, there are a few people whose voices stand out due to their determination and optimism. Their attitude and words stand out because they are counter to the prevailing sentiment of the public, fellow citizens, and the world. Dr. King projected his unique optimism after many years of devoting his life to civil rights for blacks and facing withering criticism and death threats. He was assassinated the day after delivering his "I've been to the mountaintop speech," but his optimistic words gave comfort and purpose to the civil rights movement that still resonates today.

Unfortunately, people are too easily drawn to negativity and focus on the bad things. Perhaps it is a coping mechanism; a way for people to rationalize what they think is inevitable.

Ultimately, it is often the easiest path—to accept defeat or the will of others—than to resist, to believe in a brighter future.

That is why those persons who fail to accept defeatism—who fail to accept the status quo; who see that there is an alternative to what is in front of them—those are truly remarkable persons.

President Abraham Lincoln, in the aftermath of the bloody battle of Gettysburg where more than 45,000 soldiers were killed or wounded, provided the nation a succinct-yet-powerful message as the public wondered how long the carnage would continue. President Lincoln's finished his remarks by saying: *"...that we here highly resolve that these dead shall not have died in vain—that this nation, under God, shall have a new birth of freedom— and that government of the people, by the people, for the people, shall not perish from the earth".*

In the "Gettysburg Address," President Lincoln not only honored those brave soldiers who fought at the battle, but was also able to remain focused on what he saw would be the eventual outcome of the Civil War...a new birth of freedom. That ideal was probably not obvious to many in the country at the time, but Lincoln's prevailing optimism that the outcome of the war would lead to a stronger democracy and nation helped give new buoyancy to the country as it moved toward the conclusion of the war.

While we can take inspiration from historical figures such as Rev. Dr. Martin Luther King Jr. and Abraham Lincoln, it is not just those epic figures from history who are the brave voices of optimism in the face of challenge. It could be the volunteer at a local homeless shelter who believes we can help combat homelessness one person at time and who doesn't back down from the daunting task. It can be the co-worker who provides loving support to a family member who has cancer through selfless service in an effort to beat the terrible disease.

While we can't always expect to be the voice of optimism in times of trouble or upheaval, I challenge all of us, myself included, to pause before we succumb to negativity, and see if we can find our voice of optimism.

Pat Trudgeon

Education: B.A., international relations; M.S., urban and regional planning, University of Wisconsin-Madison

Work: City manager, City of Roseville, Minnesota, since 2013; community development director, City of Roseville, six years. Previously, community development director, City of Ramsey, MN; planning and development director, City of North Branch, MN; worked for the Wisconsin State Legislature and for a Wisconsin-based lobbying firm; Beloit, WI, city council in the early 1990s.

Book: *Flags of Our Fathers* by James Bradley with Ron Powers

Quote: Whatever you are, be a good one —Abraham Lincoln

Very little is needed to make a happy life.
It is all within yourself—in your way of thinking.
MARCUS AURELIUS

Optimism—A Critical Trait

Craig Waldron

So what traits help create a rewarding and successful life? Optimism is certainly one of them!

I often find myself wondering what the basic traits and characteristics are that help people live a successful, positive life. After over 41 years of working in public service as well as teaching at Hamline University for a number of years, I have observed roughly seven traits that I believe are critical and extremely helpful as we travel through life.

The first, of course, relates to what we are all about in our Optimist Club. It is crucial that people have a positive attitude and optimistic outlook on life. They, in turn, reinforce this perspective through seeking out others with a positive, hopeful outlook on life, which reinforces their perspective. For example, after 40 years in public service, I am still extremely optimistic about the role of government and how it can improve people's lives. This has been reinforced by my public-sector colleagues and my fellow professors.

Secondly, successful people have confidence that they control their life and their own destiny. They do not ring their hands and rely on Providence—they create their future. They also realize they have a choice as to how they react to certain events in life and how they respond to them. They are not victims.

Third, truly successful people are willing to help others and respect others, particularly those who can do nothing for them. This is a true sign of empathy and civility.

Next successful people show significant resiliency to life's challenges. They learn from mistakes and setbacks and show the characteristics of "grit."

Successful people have a high degree of emotional intelligence. This has been shown, along with grit, to have a higher correlation to success in life compared to the traditional IQ.

Successful people show an insatiable degree of curiosity. They want to learn about anything and everything. Learning does not stop for them after graduation.

Last of all, they are grateful. They truly appreciate all that surrounds them and the positive life they live.

So many of these characteristics are present and reinforced in our Optimist Club. It is important to point out that yes, we are optimistic, but we are not Pollyannas. We understand and live by the Stockdale Paradox which exhibits optimism that is tempered by a clear understanding of reality. That is an important combination for a positive life!

Success is not the key to happiness.
Happiness is the key to success.
If you love what you are doing, you will be successful.
ALBERT SCHWEITZER

Craig Waldron

Education: B.A., sociology, University of Iowa; M.A, urban studies, Minnesota State University-Mankato; Ph.D., public administration, Hamline University

Work: Lecturer, Hamline University and city manager of North St. Paul. Formerly community development director, Roseville, and city administrator, Oakdale, MN.

Book: *Astrophysics for People in a Hurry* by Neil deGrasse Tyson

Quote: We can't predict the future but we can create it! —Peter Drucker

More: https://www.linkedin.com/in/dr-craig-waldron-622059a

No act of kindness, no matter how small, is ever wasted.
AESOP

Speakers

*In the midst of winter, I found there was, within me,
an invincible summer.*

ALBERT CAMUS

SPEAKERS

Paul Anderson
Dave Durenberger
Cindra Kamphoff
Steve Kloyda
David McNally
Denny Sanford
Dave Unmacht
Robert Veninga*
Kit Welchlin
Scott Welle*
*Member
....
Emily Parker

The Pursuit of Optimism in a Cynical Era

Justice Paul H. Anderson (Retired)

The Roseville Area Optimist Club, a civic group founded on the idea that having a positive attitude and mindset is key to success, has asked me to talk about their core belief—optimism. I am to address how to look for it and how to recognize it. I will do my best to say something that furthers the club's mission.

A Cynical Time

Friends say I have a Pollyanna-like attitude toward life; that I view the proverbial glass of life two-thirds full rather than half-full or half empty. This attitude serves me well. But, to tell a painful truth, this attitude is difficult to sustain in today's cynical era. We are a polarized society and are increasingly becoming a nation of cynics. Cynical mindsets are a reason why we need the Optimists more than ever.

Cynic and skeptic are words often linked with each other, but they are different. Being skeptical is important to an informed citizen. Skepticism is a useful tool when seeking truth and asking, "Why." Skepticism means being curious, sometimes relentlessly curious, in asking why things are the way they appear, or why they are the way you tell me they are.

Cynicism is a dangerous trait in a democratic society. The word cynic comes from Greek philosophers who promoted a worldview based on doubt, mistrust, suspicion, and disbelief. A cynic believes that people are motivated by self-interest, not the common good. A cynic distrusts and is suspicious of fellow citizens and the institutions that allow a civil society to function well. When cynicism flourishes, ordinary people often become angry and resentful.

Anger and Resentment

Cynical attitudes poison society and undermine our liberty. Pankaj Mishra, in *Age of Anger: A History of the Present,* writes that changes during the past few decades have resulted in, "… a tremendous increase in mutual hatred and a somewhat universal irritability of everybody against everybody else, or *resentment*—an existential resentment of other people's being, caused by an intense mix of envy and sense of humiliation and powerlessness."

Mishra notes that anger and resentment are global phenomena, not an isolated event that surfaced during the 2016 presidential election. Anger and resentment are often the result of economic insecurity, marginalization, and a feeling of being left out. Anger and resentment are so pervasive that one can surmise we are living through one of the most dangerous times in American history.

Shaping Our Future

A different view of the future we face includes hope and optimism. This view takes some hard work and discipline. It is a view disparaged and dismissed by cynics; nevertheless, I firmly believe in it.

There is room for hope and optimism when we appreciate what it means to have an uncertain future. You may be skeptical about my belief and want me to explain and justify it. I will try to do so. Hope and optimism in the future can be found in the phrase "an uncertain future." If the future is uncertain, we have the ability do something about it. Hope and optimism exist because of uncertainty. When the future is uncertain, we can have an impact on it.

We are not like an 18th-century Russian serf whose life was certain, dismal, and devoid of hope and optimism. The good news about the uncertainties we face in our lives is that we have options. We can do something about uncertainty. Our lives are not certain, dismal, and devoid of hope and optimism. We can put ourselves in a position to shape and control the future in a positive manner.

Doing the Right Thing

We live in a land of opportunity. Our founders envisioned a society in which we provide the maximum opportunity for the maximum number of people to achieve happiness. To pursue this goal, they gave us a remarkable amount of freedom to influence what we can do. We play a key role in designing of our own future. Hope and optimism should come with having such power.

But there is a catch. If we are going to have an impact on an uncertain future, we must, by word and deed, employ positive attitudes that cause us to interact with all aspects of society to make it better. We must comprehend why Optimist Clubs need to educate the public about the rules of engagement for shaping an uncertain future. Optimists are all about helping us to do the right thing. This objective is a cornerstone of your mission. Following the rules for the success you espouse, we can face that future with hope and optimism.

Rules of Engagement

I intend to outline some traits and actions that can enable us to shape the future and nurture hope and optimism.

An Open Mind

An open mind and a willingness to embrace change is essential. Change is inevitable. We need to be part of it and shape it. We cannot afford to operate from a myopic notion that change will not happen. We all know people who do not want change. Adherents to this position often nurture a view of the past that is a fantasy vision of how great it used to be. Robert Kennedy described this thinking when he said: "… there are people in every time and every land who want to stop history in its tracks. They fear the future, mistrust the present, and invoke the security of a comfortable past which, in fact, never existed."

Often those who oppose change feel economically insecure. A business or occupation they devoted their lives to is going away. They feel a loss of power or marginalized by the rest of society because of increased workplace competition from women, persons of color, and immigrants. Circumstances drive them to have an unrealistic, nostalgic attitude toward the past. That we elected a black president who, they wrongly believe, allowed others—those different from themselves—to cut ahead, "to jump the line," only intensified their anger and resentment. They have come to believe that hard work is no longer enough for them to succeed and that they are powerless to change their destiny. These attitudes drain hope and optimism from their lives.

Most things in the past were not all that great, at least not for everyone. History shows that things were not that good for working women, persons of color, persons with disabilities, and many others who found themselves on the fringes of society. There was a discernible lack of shared humanity and concern for persons in certain parts of society. The good old days for which many have a nostalgic yearning did not exist. Further, during the "good old days," we often failed to fulfill our founders' mandate to provide the maximum opportunity for the maximum number of people to achieve happiness.

A person should not identify with the cynic who nostalgically sits on the sidelines of life and vents anger and resentment to anyone who will listen. Rather, a wise citizen should accept the idea that society is always changing and seek ways to make life better for everyone. The sooner each of us gets on board and embraces this philosophy, the more hopeful and optimistic we will be.

Show Up for Opportunities

If hope and optimism are important to us, they will not be found if we sit on the sidelines. Be ready, willing, and able to "show up" for opportunity. I have had the privilege of teaching abroad in several different countries. Every time I come back home, I discover that I am more enthralled with the democratic society we have created. American democracy is not the only kind of democracy that works. It is unwise to believe we can export our unique system around the world lock, stock, and barrel. American democracy does not work well everywhere. But it is a system that has worked well for us for over two centuries. We must cherish it, understand its strengths and weaknesses, and be diligent in our efforts to preserve it.

America is called the "Land of Opportunity." The amazing thing is that this is true. We live in a country filled with opportunity. Our obligation is to spot opportunities and to show up for them. Once we show up, we have an experience. Most times it's good; sometimes it's not so good, but we can learn life lessons from bad experiences.

A bad experience shaped me for the better. It was a surprising defeat in a school board election. I believed I had done a good job and deserved to be reelected. I was devastated by the defeat, but I learned many lessons from it. They were: To always do what you believe is right and not to expend too much time looking over your shoulder to see what others may be doing to thwart your goals and lead to what you think might be your undoing. It does not matter that much. I learned that there is life after defeat if doing what you believed is right is what led to defeat. This unexpected election defeat strengthened my understanding that I must always be true to myself. It is a belief that served me well when I was Supreme Court Justice.

Other lessons learned from showing up are: An increased self-confidence, a better understanding of ourselves and others, insight into how the world works, knowledge of institutions and systems, and a better ability to perceive and analyze what's happening to us. We also gain the ability to spot other opportunities, to learn from them, and to gain the ability to discern good opportunities from bad.

Luck, Preparation, and Opportunity
Understanding another concept helps us live hopeful and optimistic lives. This concept is luck. Be prepared for luck be a part of your life. Luck can have much to do with being hopeful, successful, and optimistic. But remember what the Roman statesman Seneca said about luck: Luck happens when preparation meets opportunity.

Preparation enables us to be lucky when opportunity presents itself. A positive attitude enables us to be prepared for opportunity when it presents itself. I consider myself to be a lucky person. Looking back on my life, I see that my approach to life enabled me to do the things that prepared me for opportunity when it presented itself. I have been lucky because I showed up for opportunity and was prepared to take advantage of it. That old Scout motto works—Be Prepared.

Pursuing Happiness

"Pursuit of happiness" is a theory of governance advocated by our founders. It recognizes that government cannot make everybody happy and that it cannot be the first resort for solving all of society's problems. But government has a very important role. It provides the platform for us to work together to provide the maximum opportunity for the maximum number of citizens to achieve happiness.

Acting collectively, we provide for our mutual safety, i.e., a military, police, fire, and first-responder protection, etc. We provide access to education so that we do not waste the mind of a single person. We provide infrastructure such as roads, railroads, air transportation, telecommunications, high-speed internet, etc. Jointly constructed infrastructure allows us to live better lives. Access to good healthcare may be something else we can provide to make our society better. Our mutual happiness depends on us working together so that everyone has the maximum opportunity to achieve happiness. How we achieve this collective goal is left up to us. The burden to succeed rests squarely on our shoulders—yours and mine.

Taking Risks

Do not be afraid to take calculated risks. Our reach should exceed our grasp. Have the ability to dream and to be open to the mysteries of life. Retain a childlike sense of wonder and the ability to always seek more knowledge. Curiosity pursued with a passion is essential to taking risks, having dreams, and seeking knowledge. The wonder curiosity inspires promotes a positive attitude along with hope and optimism. Curiosity causes us to use that important word *why.* Curiosity can intentionally, and sometimes unintentionally, permit us to discover ways to control and shape a better future.

Getting Lost

Being curious and taking risks may have unexpected consequences, such as occasionally getting lost. Today, getting lost is hard to do. We live in an age of Google Maps in which Siri and other computer personalities direct us where to go. But the type of lost that Siri can help with is not the type of getting lost that I am talking about.

Take the risk of getting lost that comes with stepping outside the envelope of conventional thinking; outside our comfort zone. Step off the well-traveled route and explore the unknown. When we do, we are likely to meet people we normally do not associate with. They can teach us unexpected things. Getting lost keeps us open to learning, to appreciate, and even look forward to a chance encounter with another person—to be surprised by their thinking and the worlds they inhabit.

We can develop empathy for others by seeing them as they are, learning from them, and understanding their dreams. Even confronting someone's suffering can help us to confront some of our own uncertainty about the future. We can gain self-confidence from each other because our shared knowledge often reveals how much we have in common. By sharing with others, we can become more hopeful and optimistic as we appreciate the mysteries and wonders of the world we inhabit.

Adversity

Taking risks opens us up to adversity. The prospect of adversity may stand in the way of our ability to be hopeful and optimistic. But adversity can actually be good for us. It can teach us. Here is an example from history.

Franklin D. Roosevelt and Adlai Stevenson were prominent 20th-century Democratic politicians with national ambitions. They had similar family backgrounds. They both wanted to be President, but only FDR was. Roosevelt suffered a serious life-threatening illness. He contracted polio and was paralyzed. He endured a long road toward recovery, but while on this journey, he took upon himself the job of cheering up other similarly situated people. He wanted to give these depressed people some hope and optimism about the future. In doing so, he regained his own hope and optimism for the future.

FDR's adverse experience reshaped him into a person who was able to teach himself to be hopeful and optimistic about the future in the face of disaster. As a result, he was able to lead our country through its worst economic depression. Stevenson did not experience much adversity. There was something lacking in him that FDR had. Historians often say Stevenson was FDR without the polio given that he did not know true adversity. Adversity taught and reshaped FDR for the better. It can often do the same for us.

Failure

Fear of failure can also be a teacher. Do not fear failure; it can be a step on the road to success. Teddy Roosevelt was an extraordinary person. But he encountered and overcame many failures during his life. He repeatedly noted how much he learned from failure and the resilience it instilled in him. The same is true of other great persons such as Leonardo de Vinci and Winston Churchill. Taking risks in life means the risk of failure, but failure, in retrospect, may be a milestone on the road to success.

A Healthy Ego, Self-Doubt, and Humility

A healthy ego is an important ingredient for a positive attitude and mindset. Some people are prone to criticize ego. I am not among them. To achieve success and accomplish great things, you have to have a healthy ego. You need to like and respect yourself. Having a healthy ego does not mean being arrogant, self-important, or having the need to boost yourself up by treating others badly.

But ego needs to be tempered by self-doubt and humility. Self-doubt does not mean an inability to make decisions. I am talking about a type of open mindedness that can only come with enough humility to entertain the type of self-examination that comes with self-doubt. The quality of self-doubt allows a person to continually question his or her decisions, values, and ideals. These qualities can motivate us to be better people.

Freedom—Not "Just Another Word for Nothing Left to Lose"

We must diligently preserve our freedom. Often people are too willing to sacrifice the freedoms that grant us opportunity. To be hopeful and optimistic, we need to relentlessly and wisely defend of our freedom. Relevant lyrics from the song, *Me and Bobby McGee,* help make my point:

> *Freedom is just another word for nothin' left to lose.*
> *Feelin' good is good enough for you and me,*
> *Feelin' good is enough for me and my Bobby McGee.*

Freedom is **not** "just another word for nothing left to lose." It is a word for having everything to lose. Feeling good is **not** "good enough for you or for me" when that means losing our freedom. If we want hope and optimism, we must be free to pursue them. We must preserve our precious freedom to pursue those goals.

Justice Paul H. Anderson

Education: B.A., cum laude, political science (minors in history and economics), Macalaster College; J.D., University of Minnesota Law School

Work: VISTA (Volunteers in Service to America) volunteer attorney; special assistant attorney general, State of Minnesota; private practice of law LeVander, Gillen & Miller, South St. Paul; 1992 appointed Chief Judge, Minnesota Court of Appeals, and in 1994 Associate Justice, Minnesota Supreme Court (1994-2013).

Book: *Leonardo de Vinci* by Walter Isaacson, *Theodore Roosevelt's Darkest Journey—The River of Doubt* by Candice Millard, *Destiny of the Republic* by Candice Millard

Quote: A discriminating irreverence is the creator and protector of human liberty. —Mark Twain

You Need a Purpose

Senator Dave Durenberger

"You don't need a job, Dave, you need a purpose!"

"To know, love and serve God with your whole heart, soul, mind and strength…"

I've raised four sons who are fathers to 10 of my grandchildren who range from 12 to 23 years of age. Starting at age 16 or 17, they are asked to get serious about, "What's next? Or, what about college?" Grandpa is assumed to love them dearly, to perhaps be a source of financial support if needed, but he's not always asked, "What should I do?" When I *am* asked, I know he/she expects me to ask, "What do you want to do or to be? A teacher, analytics expert, nurse, doctor, artist?"… And sometimes I do ask just that.

But first I tell her/him the question that I was asked at age 36 by a distinguished Minnesota businessman and former governor who wanted me to work with him in his business. He knew I had just lost my wife, the mother of my four sons, to cancer. And I was about to lose my job as executive assistant to another governor of Minnesota who chose to serve just one term. This is the question he asked me that I've never forgotten—the question I choose now to ask my grandchildren about career and job choices:

"Dave," he said, *"you don't need a job. You need a purpose in your life."*

"What's that mean, Grandpa? Purpose?"

You know that I have spent much of my life in the "service" business—making it possible for other people to meet the needs assured them by life and citizenship in this community, state, and country. My service has been helping run the state of Minnesota as assistant to a governor and the country as a U.S. Senator, teaching at the University of St. Thomas' graduate School of Business, and serving on the Hennepin County Park Reserve District Board of Directors and the National Institute of Health Policy.

"Yup, Grandpa, Dad tells us that all the time about you. But 'purpose,' Grandpa? What are you talking about?"

OK, let me tell you a story from my time in the U.S. Senate. I chose to bring Minnesota ideas to Washington—ideas to improve the lives of everyone. Ideas for making healthcare and education and the environment better, more accessible, and more affordable for everyone. For 16 years I worked to improve grade- and high-school education for every kid in America, regardless of the learning disabilities or challenges they brought to school. So I asked the same question of every public school teacher I met about education reform: "When was the last day you can recall waking up in the morning and feeling as though you couldn't wait to get to school?"

I want you to believe that in all those years, not once did I get an answer to that question! Never. From any teacher. Teaching had become a source of income graded by rules and the adequacy of public financing. Not a *profession*. It had become a *"job,"* not a *"purpose!"* I wanted to change that. Because of the advice a famous governor gave me at a critical time in my life, I could. I had the power to convince others that teaching should be a *profession*—like medicine; where a sense of purpose—to heal, to make healthy—drives kids to spend an awful lot of money to get a good education so they can save lives.

For teachers, it means to *change* lives, to save lives, to *give* life to kids *and* to teachers; a reason to get up in the morning! I enjoyed that "purpose" in my life every day of my professional-service career in government. *And*, I continue to enjoy it in "retirement." Just one more thought about why I need a purpose in my life. Most Americans believe as I do that faith in God gives meaning and purpose to our lives. No doubt about it. Most learn about God as members of one religion or another. There are many. But only one God and one faith and one purpose: *"To know, love, and serve God with your whole heart, soul, mind, and strength, and your neighbor as yourself."* Service to others is the best work of life. Rather than just something to do, it is the next best thing in life to happiness!

Dave Durenberger

Education: I went to elementary, high school, and college at St. John's University, Collegeville, Minnesota; J.D., University of Minnesota

Work: Six years in U.S. Army (retired as a Captain); LeVander, Gillen, Miller and Durenberger Law Firm; executive secretary to Governor Harold LeVander; counsel for legal and community affairs, H. B. Fuller Company; U.S. Senate 1978-1995; Opus College of Business, University of St. Thomas, St. Paul, Minnesota.

Book: *American Nations: A History of the Eleven Rival Regional Cultures of North America* by Colin Woodard

Quote: The sign of God is that you will be led where you do not expect to go. —Self

What if Life Happens *For* You,
Not *To* You?

Cindra Kamphoff

I've learned a lot about optimism through running. I can remember vividly the conversations I'd have with my parents around the kitchen table after every race or track meet in high school. I loved those conversations. They helped me focus on what I learned from my last race and kept me dreaming big about what I could accomplish. They'd always ask me, "What do you want to do next, Cindra?"

Those optimistic conversations with my parents helped me win an Iowa high school state championship my senior year in 1994. I ran the fastest mile in the state that year thanks to the optimistic perspective my parents helped instill.

After pursuing my Ph.D. and having two boys, I decided to get back into running. I love the feeling of accomplishment after the run. It's also a time I can just focus on me. I do my best thinking on a run.

The marathon is my favorite race because of how much discipline it takes to train, and then how difficult it is to stay mentally strong and optimistic during the race. Wow, that can be hard! The marathon is a true test of mental and physical strength.

On April 15, 2013, I experienced the biggest test of this optimistic perspective. That date I completed my third Boston

Marathon. The Boston Marathon is my favorite because of many reasons. You feel like a rock star because thousands of people are cheering your name along the course or telling you how strong you look.

I also like the Boston Marathon because it is a challenge. The first thirteen miles, all downhill, tear at your quads and cause serious discomfort. The second thirteen miles include five big hills, most notably Heartbreak Hill around mile 21. Those are 26.2 tough miles. You must put in the work to dominate the race.

At that 2013 marathon, I crushed it. I owned the course. I pushed up Heartbreak Hill steady and strong, passing more than 100 people. I finished with my personal-best time.

As I walked back to my hotel, two blocks from the finish on Boylston Street, I had a huge, shiny smile plastered on my face. Then, the significance of the race faded into the background. I heard sirens. Then I learned why: Two bombs exploded near the finish line, killing three people and injuring an estimated 264 others, including fourteen who required amputations. From my hotel room window, I could see the terror of the bombs.

Hadn't I just crossed the same finish line—the same spot where the bombs were detonated—only fifty-five minutes earlier? It didn't seem real. I crowded around the hotel TV with my husband and our closest running friends to watch the news. We heard there might be more bombs along the course. We wondered if there could be bombs near us, or even in our hotel. We were only a few blocks from where the explosions had occurred.

I wondered if I was ever going to get home to see my two boys, Carter and Blake, who were ages three and five at the time. I forced myself to take several deep breaths and not go to the worst-case scenario. It was hard.

In that hotel room, as I sat watching news reports on that terrorist attack and the manhunt that followed, I went to some deep places. I found myself asking three pivotal questions:

Why am I here?

What difference am I making in this world?

Why do I do what I do?

I sat in the hotel room and thought about my "why," questioning if I was truly following my calling and wondering about my purpose on this earth. "Have I truly been living my calling?" I asked myself. I came to the conclusion that I was not.

When I got home, I gave my boys the biggest hug I've ever hugged in my life. I didn't feel quite like myself for a few months. It was tough to be around loud noises and I was more emotional. Being at the Boston Marathon bombing shook me to the core.

But that day was a turning point in my life. After that, I started making different decisions with my time, energy, and mindset. I started living, thinking, and performing intentionally. I started owning my why. I started to believe that everything happens *for* me, not *to* me.

There are many things I wouldn't have done in my life if I had not been in the middle of a terrorist attack that April afternoon. I would not be a leading sport psychology professional working with the Minnesota Vikings, nor would I have sought opportunities to speak to and work with some of the nation's leading companies such as Target, Nationwide, or Verizon Wireless. I would not have written my book, *Beyond Grit: Ten Powerful Practices to Gain the High-Performing Edge*.

Being at the Boston Marathon bombing woke me up to my life and forced me to think about choosing to adopt an optimistic perspective despite difficulties. When the worst things are happening around you, what do you do?

When you suffer a deep, gut-wrenching loss or are forced to change direction either at work or at home, how do you remain resilient, optimistic, and in control?

When you find yourself in the middle of change and conflict, do you have the power to see life happening *for* you, not *to* you?

I first heard Tony Robbins say this: "Everything happens *for* you, not *to* you." I attend a Tony Robbins event about once a year to help me stay optimistic and dreaming big about my goals. It's my mental fuel. After doing research about the quote, I believe author, Bryon Katie, is the first to use this phrase.

"Everything happens *for* you, not *to* you." I've found that this is one of the secrets of the world's top performers. The world's best see that the difficulties that occur can lead them on a course necessary for success. They see difficulties as their way to rise above and get ahead.

Difficulties show you how strong you are; how persistent you are. They help you understand your true potential and power. In my case, the difficulty showed me my purpose.

Ask any gold medalist, top entrepreneur, or game-changer how they overcome the impossible and defeat the unthinkable, and they will tell you that it's all in their perspective. They will tell you an optimistic perspective is essential.

When you see difficulties—such as change or adversity as being *for* you, not *to* you—you rise above and see that what you are experiencing is happening as a benefit to you. Perhaps it's happening to help you do what you were designed to do. Or teach you what is important in your life. Or show you how much grit and persistence you have.

My wish for you is that next time you experience a difficulty, change, or adversity, that you see it as happening *for* you, not *to* you. If you do, you will experience more energy, passion, and optimism.

You can repeat this Power Phrase to help remind you: I am an optimist! I see difficulties as happening *for* me, not *to* me.

Cindra Kamphoff

Education: B.A., psychology, University of Northern Iowa; M.S. and Ph.D., sport and performance psychology, University of North Carolina at Greensboro

Work: Professional speaker, coach, and author; CEO, Mentally Strong Consulting; professor, Minnesota State University, Mankato; author of *Beyond Grit: Ten Powerful Practices to Gain the High-Performing Edge*; podcaster, High Performance Mindset.

Book: *Success Principles: How to Get From Where You Are to Where You Want to Go* by Jack Canfield

Quote: If your dreams aren't scary, they aren't big enough. —Donna Williams

More: CindraKamphoff.com, mentallystrongconsulting.com For High Performance Mindset podcast episodes, search for the title on Itunes, Stitcher Radio, or iHeartRadio.

In the Beginning

Steve Kloyda

I loved art from the time I was a small boy, and my dream was to be a great artist. My belief was that I was born to create artistic ideas that would inspire, encourage, and empower others.

After graduating from the Minneapolis College of Art and Design in June of 1980, my wife Jane and I moved to Rosemount, Minnesota, a small city about 30 minutes south of Minneapolis. We moved in with her brother, Mike, who was living in an old, beat-up farm house on 100 acres of prime land. The rent was really cheap—$75 per month plus utilities for all three of us.

And so the journey began.

As the summer was coming to an end and the leaves on the trees were starting to change colors, it was time to get serious about what I was going to do next. Unfortunately, I really didn't have a clue. At this point, becoming a great artist was not part of the plan, and combined with a variety of other reasons (a long story for another book—stay tuned), I decided to take a different path.

November brought cold and snow. Months had passed since graduation. Still not sure what I wanted to do, I got in the car and drove to the unemployment office in Rosemount. Little did I realize, that cold November day would be a turning point. My life has never been the same.

While at the unemployment office, I saw an ad that read, "Stockbroker—will train. Call Tom 338-1300." Did I know anything about being a stockbroker? Absolutely not! What did it have to do with art? Absolutely nothing...or so I thought. (Paul Gauguin, the great French Post-Impressionist painter, had been a stockbroker for 10 years before he left that life to become a full-time artist. But I didn't know that at the time.)

My life was at an all-time low at that point, so I thought, "Why not? What do I have to lose?" There was only one way to go, and that was up.

I took the ad and sat down with an employment counselor to discuss the job. She took the ad, called Tom, and set up an interview for the following day. I drove home in a state of shock. What had I just gotten myself into? Frankly, I was terrified.

I was about to go into the world of business, a world with which I was totally unfamiliar. I didn't own a business suit. I didn't even own an overcoat. I had a well-worn brown leather bomber jacket and some bib overalls.

However, I did own one suit. It was white. My wife bought it for me to wear at graduation from the Minneapolis College of Art and Design. She bought it because she knew I was inspired by the white suit that John Lennon wore on the cover of *Abbey Road*. Which by the way, was one of the Beatles' finest albums.

Okay, so picture this: It's November in Minnesota. There is snow on the ground and it's cold. I am going on a job interview to become a stockbroker while wearing a white suit, and I don't own a winter dress coat. So I came up with what I thought was a great idea: I'd wear my long underwear underneath the suit to keep warm. Made sense to me.

The following morning I got up early, put on my long underwear and white suit, hopped in my truck and drove toward Minneapolis and a place where I could catch a bus to downtown. So there I was, standing in the freezing cold, wearing a white suit while waiting for a bus. I was ready to take on the world.

The bus finally arrived after about 10 minutes. I stepped aboard, paid the fare, and looked for a seat. I was met by a bus-load of staring faces, and I knew what they were thinking: "Who wears a white suit in Minnesota in November? This guy must be nuts!" And judging by my appearance, they weren't far off.

After a brief-but-uncomfortable bus ride, I got off at Nicollet and 7th Street and walked a couple of blocks to the Cargill Building, rode the elevator up to the 16th floor, and found the office of Van Clemens & Company. I walked in, introduced myself to Joanne, the receptionist, and said I was there for an interview with Tom Vanyo. She asked me to have a seat. After about 10 minutes, she escorted me to Tom's office.

I will never forget what happened next. I reached out to shake Tom's hand and my long underwear came out from under my shirt. Had he noticed? How could he not? There was a full two inches of it! But Tom never said a word. We both sat down and the interview began.

From the very start, Tom really inspired me. He was excited and passionate about life. He told me about all the opportunities and the potential to become highly successful. I soaked it up like a sponge.

Then came the one defining moment for me. Tom said, "All you have to do every day is call people on the telephone and *paint a picture* in their mind of the potential investment opportunity." It was like the heavens opened up and the angels began to sing. In that moment, *I got it*! I could see it.

I had spent 20 years painting pictures. Now it was time to paint word pictures. I knew I could do this, and be very successful at it. I begged Tom for the job. He hired me on the spot and so began a new adventure that would shape my life to this day.

Within my first eight months, I opened up 180 new accounts from cold calls. Each month I set a record on the most new accounts opened. I was on fire and I never looked back.

I discovered that I loved to prospect. I couldn't wait to get in the office every day and make calls. I was motivated. When the weekend came, I couldn't wait until Monday to get back on the phone. Each day was a new adventure.

Two nights a week I prospected from the old farm house in Rosemount. I would huddle up next to the wood-burning stove (yes, that was one source of heat along with an oil burner which wasn't very reliable), and dial the phone (yes, it was an old rotary dial phone).

Many times I remember my wife, Jane, saying to me, "If I hear that pitch one more time..." And, "Throw another log on the fire while you are at it."

That was my birth as a professional salesperson. I discovered that I loved everything about sales...especially prospecting. I became fascinated by the entire sales process, but it was prospecting that really lit my fire.

One simple idea has changed my life, inspired me over the years, and profoundly contributed to my success in sales: The law of sowing and reaping. It's a basic truth. You reap exactly what you sow in life. You reap nothing more and nothing less.

A person is a success simply because he or she has made the effort and put in the time behind the plow to become a success. I have probably made more sales calls during my lifetime than most. It's not a matter of me wanting to brag or even to win some phantom competition; I simply want to illustrate a point. The only reason that I have any success in my life is because I have made the commitment to sow as many seeds and as many opportunities as possible. And there is absolutely nothing—and I do mean nothing—stopping you from doing the same thing.

There have been many days that were extremely difficult. It hasn't always been easy. Starting a sales career in 1980 and then starting my business in 1990 were the hardest things I've ever done.

Without trying to force my belief system on you, I simply want to share something I read that has encouraged me throughout the years. I'll paraphrase it.

In the beginning, God said, "Let there be light" and there was light. Then for the next six days, whatever God said happened. Then all of a sudden, in Genesis, chapter 2:8, it reads, "The Lord planted a garden eastward in Eden."

It didn't say, "God said, 'Let there be a garden.'" I was shocked when I read that for the first time. Why didn't God speak the garden into existence? He could have, but He didn't.

I was so inspired by that. There it was, a simple-but-powerful Daily Prospecting Plan. All I had to do each day was plant a seed (my solution) in the mind of a prospect or customer, and He would make it grow.

That mere act of planting a few seeds produced one of the most beautiful gardens that the world has ever seen. So why couldn't I (or you) plant a few seeds with a few phone calls, emails, Tweets, etc., and produce something truly beautiful as well?

Do you know how hard it would be to make a tree? It's not within my power, for sure. But, I do have the power to plant a seed, water it, nourish it, and watch it grow.

A typical farmer will go out in the springtime and plant his or her crop. How crazy would it be for that farmer to go out two weeks after he planted and begin to curse the ground because it hasn't produced? That wouldn't happen, because the farmer knows that it takes time to grow a crop.

Also, when does the farmer prepare and plant? In the springtime; fall is far too late. But I see that mistake all the time with salespeople. They wait too long to plant and there is no crop to harvest in the fall.

A farmer plans not only for a future harvest but for potential challenges as well. Let's say the farmer starts with 100 acres to plant. The farmer knows that aside from any natural disaster, there will be a certain amount of crops to harvest in the fall. This is simply the way it works.

The farmer knows that after planting, the birds will eat some of the seed. The farmer also knows that the hot summer sun will scorch some of the plants. The farmer also knows that the weeds will infiltrate the ground and choke out some of the plants. But the farmer is confident that there will be a harvest. The farmer is also wise enough to plant more than he needs.

What does this have to do with sales? *Everything!* Like the farmer, we reap exactly what we sow. Having observed thousands of salespeople over the years, one of the biggest reasons salespeople fail is that they don't plant enough seeds. They clearly don't understand the law of sowing and reaping. By the time the birds, sun, and weeds are finished, there's not much left for the farmer to harvest.

Sales is the easiest job in the world if you are disciplined and work hard at it. Plant your seeds, tend to your plants, and you will reap the harvest.

The more prospecting attempts you make, the more contacts you will make, and the more meaningful conversations you will have. And when you do that, it leads to more (and better!) sales.

Let me leave you with a quote from Jim Rohn that has helped shaped my life throughout the years, "Work harder on yourself than you do on your job and your gifts will always make a room for you."

Be Blessed!

Steve

Steve Kloyda

Education: Graduated from Vocational Institute, graphic design; B.A., fine art, Minneapolis College of Art and Design

Work: Stockbroker; founded Telemasters; rebranded company to The Prospecting Expert, Inc.

Book: *The Five Major Pieces to the Life Puzzle* by Jim Rohn

Quote: What lies behind you and what lies in front of you, pales in comparison to what lies inside is you. —Ralph Waldo Emerson

More: TheProspectingExpert.com
Get In The Door Podcast: iTunes
steve@theprospectingexpert.com

Confidence—
The Foundation of Success

David McNally

When my eldest daughter reached the age of sixteen, I became abruptly aware of my primary role as a parent. It happened as she was preparing to get her driver's license. Like any parent, I had my fears, but they were quickly allayed when the driving instructor said, "Don't be concerned; your daughter is very confident."

I have since realized that there is no other single quality that more affects the outcomes of our lives than confidence. Only with confidence do we advance boldly in the direction of our dreams. Only with confidence do we tackle life's challenges with the faith that we can handle them. There is no greater gift that a parent can imbue in a child than confidence.

This is not, however, a quality that is rampant in the world. In these extraordinary times of change and opportunity, some people are exclaiming, "What a fantastic time to be alive!" Others, however, are mired in the self-defeating game of, "Ain't it awful!" Confidence plays a key role in which perspective we choose.

So, how do we build confidence? Here are three ideas and questions to reflect upon.

A sense of purpose

Confident people have a sense of purpose—a belief they are important, that their lives matter. With seven billion people on Planet Earth, it can be challenging to believe that there could be a special purpose for each of our lives. But nothing will have a more positive effect on your level of accomplishment and happiness than the belief that you bring to humanity something special that no one else can offer. **Question:** Why am I here?

Self-awareness

Confident people have a high level of self-awareness. They know what they are good at—their special abilities. They know that success, satisfaction and fulfillment are the rewards for contributing their gifts and talents toward something that makes a difference. **Question:** What are my top three strengths or attributes?

Commitment

Confident people know that the accomplishment of any worthwhile endeavor requires commitment. Commitment is the parent of determination, and determined action is the fuel that ignites success. Commitment is the common quality you will discover in the lives of all those who achieve their goals. **Question:** What do I value and believe in?

In a future that promises more and more change, more and more challenges, and yet more and more opportunities, it will be those who believe in themselves who will have a clear sense of what they want their futures to be and what choices they have for creating that future.

Belief in oneself does not happen, however, by chance or good luck. It is because you purposefully and deliberately, step by step, built the confidence to pursue your dreams. With confidence, therefore, a life is transformed from one where you are merely surviving to one where you are thriving.

David McNally

Education: St. Michael's College, Adelaide, Australia

Work: Founder, TransForm Corporation, 35 years.

Book: *Mark Of An Eagle—How Your Life Changes the World.* I am the author.

Quote: In order to be irreplaceable, one must always be different.
—Coco Chanel

More: www.davidmcnally.com

In order to succeed, we must first believe we can.
NIKOS KAZANTZAKIS

Aspire to Inspire Before You Expire

Denny Sanford

When I was four years old, I had the unfortunate experience of losing my mother to breast cancer. My father was a loving man who mentored me, but also worked me hard in his warehouse from age eight. He passed when I was 22 years old. I look at the loss of my parents as making me become more independent.

While I regretted having to work all the way through college nearly full time, I now understand what my father taught me. He had the same kind of life, being born on a small farm and having to share it with seven older siblings. I thank him every day.

Being born on the poor side of town added to my understanding of life and the need for hard work which I still enjoy at age 82. Along the way I had a very mean older brother and stepmother, but I learned how to deal with both of them and with life in general.

I look at life as a learning experience and continue to this day trying to understand everything. However, high-tech abilities do not come to me easily.

After high school, I became involved in a neighborhood fight due to beer consumption and was sentenced to a prison-like workhouse in St. Paul for 90 days, which was horrible. When I got an audience with the judge who sentenced me, I thanked him for my "wake up call." I told him I would go to college if he would pardon me, although I had no previous intent to do so. However, 35 days 10 hours and 15 minutes into my sentence, I was released, and graduated from the University of Minnesota with a B.A. degree in psychology. After college graduation, I personally thanked the judge again.

My grade-school years were fun at Linwood Elementary School in St Paul until third grade and at Ramsey Middle School through eighth grade. I walked to school each day for about a mile. I had many good friends, the majority of whom have passed on. High school at St. Paul Central was meaningful, as was my experience at the University of Minnesota.

Chi Psi Fraternity was very meaningful in terms of friendships and the pressure from members who stressed scholastics as much as fun. I was never a great student, but I graduated.

My business background began when I was hired by the Armstrong Cork Company as a salesman in southern Michigan for flooring products. I was extremely successful, but left after a year when the company could not reimburse me on an incentive basis after I brought them a huge account.

In my opinion, compensation should be commensurate with results, and I made Armstrong millions of dollars while making $425 per month. I was denied a $50 raise due to company policy! I left Michigan and returned to Minnesota where I married my fiancée Anne, who is a dear friend until this day, as is my other former wife Colleen.

Next, I became a manufacturer's representative on straight commission, selling commercial construction materials. After a year of success, I brought in another Armstrong Cork friend, Charlie Crowell, as an equal partner who stayed with me for three years. He left to become a stockbroker.

Eventually I started a distribution company, Contech (Construction Technology), and got into private labeling products specified by architects. I then bought a great company, Sonneborn Building Products, from Sears Roebuck, as the company did not fit well with them. That was a real coup, as I bought it right and acquired a national sales force.

Sonneborn was a forty-year old company known worldwide for great products and I expanded it significantly. In 1972, I took Contech public for $5 per share and sold it in 1982 for $35 per share, amounting to nearly $30 million dollars, of which I owned about 80%.

After a few years investing via my new company, Threshold Ventures (a venture capital company), I was approached by a dear Young Presidents' Organization friend, Steve Adams, who asked me to buy a very small bank in South Dakota to provide him funding for his divorce. I did. Today that $87-million-dollar bank is a $2-billion-dollar bank and credit-card issuer.

We do well by doing good for people who are credit-impaired. We educate them back into stronger financial standing for credit cards from larger banks that give them more credit. It is a risky business, but my strong team of associates manages the risks very well.

What have I learned along the way? Surround yourself with strong people who know what you do not know but understand and accept what you do not know! I also learned not to retire as long as I have health and keep building companies. Also, be a good person and surround yourself with honest, good people who have similar values.

I have also learned that trust and respect are foremost in both personal and business relationships, and never stray from that credo. The Young Presidents' Organization has been very meaningful to me for education, ideas exchange and world travel.

My philanthropy is primarily aimed at children and health-care matters, and there are 16 organizations and programs that bear my name. In total, I have given away in excess of $1.5 billion and have pledged more than that on my passing.

Of those that are having the greatest impact is the Sanford Harmony Project that teaches young children how to try and understand the opposite gender and how to communicate with them. Children are not normally taught that, but need to know early in life before middle school as a prevention matter to reduce conflicts and hopefully reduce divorce. This project is being taught to school kids in New York, Los Angeles and throughout the USA on my nickel. Today more than one million kids are learning Harmony and we expect that to increase to more than 30 million kids in a few years.

My family consists of two former wives who are both great friends, two great sons, and two grandsons and a granddaughter.

My hobbies are golf, sailboat racing, skiing and world travel, and I rank Carnival in Rio as the greatest event in the world to watch.

I consider myself Mr. Lucky!!!!!! Being proactive and taking risks are my nature, along with recognizing opportunities.

PMA is also important!!! Positive Mental Attitude. It goes with Mr. Lucky!

Denny Sanford

Education: B.A., psychology, University of Minnesota

Work history: Salesman for flooring products; manufacturer's rep selling construction materials; had my own distribution company for architectural products; started a venture capital company; bought a small bank in Sioux Falls, S.D., expanded it across the state and added credit-card issuing; philanthropy.

Book: *The Power of Compassion* by Dalai Lama XIV

Quote: Be kind whenever possible. It is always possible.
—The Dalai Lama XIV

A pound of pluck is worth a ton of luck.
JAMES A. GARFIELD

The Gift of Public Speaking

David Unmacht

I recall with horror, and now humor, how dreadfully nervous I used to get when I was asked to speak publicly. As a new city administrator and 24-year-old, I had little experience in front of crowds of any size, outside of classmates and friends (and they don't count). Yet, my time had come, and being a public speaker came with the job. Although I don't recall the words "public speaker" in the job description, it was far too late to contest the fine print.

Vivid memories persist of a racing heart, sweaty palms, and unchecked nerves. As a new administrator learning the business of city government, I brought limited poise, some self-confidence, and a working, but not-strong knowledge of my subject matter to my presentations. I also had essentially no experience in front of an audience, especially strangers who were judging me on my message and delivery.

But time, opportunities, and practice changed all of that and the reality is anyone can be a "good-to-great" public speaker. Numerous surveys routinely report that public speaking is a fear many people live with. But it doesn't have to be that way. The journey during my 35-plus years in my position is filled with gaffes, guffaws, and applause. Today, public speaking is second nature and I enjoy—and look forward to—opportunities to speak to audiences in all shapes and sizes.

Space limits a full disclosure of ideas, but I offer a few of the best that work well for me. I hope that you find value and wisdom in these suggestions to help you along your own personal journey. For ease of presentation and understanding, I divide this advice into three sections: Preparation, presentation, and evaluation.

First, preparation.
Nerves are not all bad; in fact, some level of anxiety can be healthy. I think pre-speech nerves reflect care and concern for wanting to do a good job. Unless of course you are unprepared, but that is your own fault. Remember, in most speeches, you know the subject matter better than your audience; this fact can be comforting. I recommend that you arrive early, review the podium or location of your presentation, and get comfortable and familiar with the room. Make sure your technology works; this may sound trite, but it is very important. Above all, practice and prepare. This is a quality we often take for granted, but when learning how to speak in public, practice, practice, practice. In my early days, I practiced speeches in front of a mirror; no kidding. Finally, before you begin, take two to four deep breaths; this really does relax you.

Second, presentation.
A simple fact is to never read directly from a script or material unless you are quoting or referencing something important. PowerPoints can be effective, but I think they are overused and often are a crutch for the speaker. If you are using technology, refer to the content, and use it to help tell your story, but always speak to your audience.

Continually scan your audience, make eye contact, and change the tone and depth of your voice to keep the audience interested, informed, and *awake*. When making a very important point, I like to say the statement twice; it is impactful for the audience to hear the same words a second time.

Third, evaluation.
When I was young, I would ask a co-worker, or sometimes someone I trusted in the audience, to listen carefully and be willing to evaluate my style and presentation. I encouraged feedback and constructive suggestions. I wanted—and still do to this day—input on how I did. It is important for me to continuously improve my skills. Did I "hit the mark"; was I "on-point"; was the audience listening; was I too long, too short, not strong enough, etc.? This feedback, especially early in my career, was so very important to learn, grow, and develop my skills.

Finally, a few overall ideas for you to consider: Always be honest. Never say anything in a speech that is not true. Bring water or something to drink if your mouth gets dry. Err on the side of brevity versus length. Tell stories or relate personal experiences; these are the most powerful messages. And be careful to avoid acronyms or jargon. There is nothing worse than a speech your audience does not understand.

For professionals in local government, you cannot avoid public speaking. Embrace it; make it your strength. You can turn your worries into pride and your fears into opportunities with deliberate preparation, presentation, and evaluation.

David Unmacht

Work: Executive Director, League of Minnesota Cities

Education: B.A., political science and business administration, Wartburg College; M.A., public administration, Drake University; attended the Senior Executive Institute at the University of Virginia.

Book: *The Obstacle is the Way* by Ryan Holiday

More: Twitter @UnmachtMnCities.

Be like the bird that, pausing in her flight awhile
on boughs too slight, feels them give way beneath her
and yet sings, knowing that she has wings.

VICTOR HUGO

My Favorite Students

Robert Veninga

I have enjoyed teaching many students at the University of Minnesota. But my favorite group was older adults coming to the University to complete their education, renew their credentials or even to start a new career. These students were passionate, engaged and focused. Their success was marked with undeniable optimism.

What enabled them to complete their education when they were twice as old as other students? What enabled them to succeed academically when engaged in busy careers, raising families and earning a living?

First, they had a dream. I recall asking a 60-year old student why he wanted to return to school. He smiled and said: "I have unfinished business. I always had a dream to be a college graduate." Here is an important observation: *The size of your optimism will be the size of your dreams.* Dream big! Poet Carl Sandburg had it right: "Nothing happens unless first a dream."

Second, when times turned tough, these mid-life professionals summoned their courage. Believe me, returning to school after 10, 20 or 30 years is not easy. I recall one 40-year old who was struggling and on the verge of hanging it up. But he did not quit. He drilled down on his experience by saying: "I have had setbacks and have overcome them. I will get through this." Indeed he did. Here is some sage advice from author Mary

Anne Radmacher: "Courage doesn't always roar. Sometimes it is the quiet voice at the end of the day saying...I will try again tomorrow."

Third, those who succeeded in achieving their academic dreams had a support system—people who loved them and cared about them—including fellow students. On many occasions, I saw young students patiently teach basic computer skills to older students. I learned a lot watching these young students, and I couldn't help but think of the Rabbis of Old who said: "If you help a single person, it's better than trying to save the world. Because if you help a single person, the likelihood of you getting something done is very great. But if you go out to save the world, you'll surely fail." If you want to achieve your dreams, make sure you have caring people in your corner.

Fourth, I learned that having a sense of humor is vital to success. One student who was barely able to get through a statistics class confided with a twinkle in his eye: "In case you are wondering, I am not going to be the class valedictorian." Mark Twain had it right: "The human race has only one really effective weapon and that is laughter."

Fifth, these mid-career professionals shared a similar characteristic: They were willing to get out of their comfort zone. Getting out of our comfort zone is one of the most difficult lessons of life. We become familiar with our routines. We stop learning. We stop listening and even reading. The result? Bill Hoogterp, quoted in *Fortune* magazine, notes: "All of us are driving a Ferrari with the hand break on." Take your hand off the break. How? Get up a little earlier in the morning and define *three* goals for the day. Determine *two* conversations you want to have. Write out *one* thing for which you are thankful.

When you do this exercise, the chances of getting out of your comfort zone dramatically increases.

Finally, the students who succeed in their academics and in their careers shared a similar characteristic: They live with gratitude. Feeling blest is a powerful motivator, for when we feel blest, we see the world differently. We perceive our families, our careers, our hopes and dreams with open eyes. Feelings of discouragement and even resentment due to life's injustices begin to fade. Author Sarah Young was correct when she noted: "A life of thankfulness becomes a life filled with miracles."

When my mid-career students received their degrees at commencement, there would be hoots and shouts and even standing ovations from family members and friends. I would sit in my seat beaming with pride, for I knew what these students sacrificed in order to achieve their dreams.

Robert Veninga

Eduction: M.A. and Ph.D., speech communications, University of Minnesota

Work: Professor Emeritus in the School of Public Health, University of Minnesota (taught for 34 years); author, speaker, active lay person in the Evangelical Lutheran Church of America.

Book: *Grit: The Power of Passion and Perseverance* by Angela Duckworth

Quote: I am an optimist. It does not seem too much use being anything else. —Winston Churchill

More: www.robertveninga.com

I've Never Been Lucky

Kit Welchlin

When I think about it, I guess I have always been an optimist. I've never been lucky, but I have always been optimistic.

I grew up relatively poor on a hog and dairy farm. However, ever since I was a child, I heard stories about people with limited resources who worked and studied hard, and overcame their challenges. I had also witnessed, firsthand, rags-to-riches stories in the small communities near where I had grown up. I observed people who started out with little, prospered personally and professionally, and rose to become respected community leaders. I learned that most people don't start out with much.

When I was in third grade, my mom and dad, who were sharecroppers, bought a farm on a contract for deed, about a mile east of where we were farming at the time. This move put me in a different school district and caused me to transfer from country school to town school. My new teacher had class elections that day and I was elected class president. A couple of years later, I learned she did that every time a new student joined her class. I learned to be humble.

The act of risk-taking demonstrated by my mom and dad, when they bought that farm, stayed with me my entire life. Taking risks and being optimistic that things would turn out just fine seemed like the way to live a life with little regret.

I think optimism was what compelled me to buy a struggling manufacturing company when I was twenty-one years old. The company grew to three companies in three states during the next six years. It wasn't easy; it was a lot of work, and I didn't make money every day—just like farming. I learned to never give up.

When I was twenty-five, I started buying "yuck" real estate. These are properties that when you drive by, you say, "Yuck!" I have always enjoyed the challenge of buying distressed property, improving it, repositioning it, and creating an asset people would want. I believe optimism gave me the vision to look past what was and to see what could be. Again, it wasn't easy; it was a lot of work, and I didn't make money with every project. I also suffered through the experience of losing my financing when the bank I had worked with for years failed during the last recession. I recovered. I learned to bank with more than one bank.

Since 1991, I have enjoyed being a professional speaker and real estate investor. When spending time with my colleagues, many of whom are motivational and inspirational speakers, I can't help but be optimistic. As a professional speaker, you must believe the information and stories you share will have a positive impact on people's lives. My presentations are well researched and well rehearsed so they will be well received. Again, being a professional speaker isn't easy; it's a lot of work, and I don't make money every day. I have learned to study and to trust my informed intuition.

To maintain my optimism over the years, I have carried along what I call my "Survival Kit." In my Franklin Planner I carry a list of ten things I'm most thankful for, a list of eighteen things I love to do, a story about a scorpion and a frog with a lesson concerning sociopaths, and my favorite picture of myself at a time in my life when I felt invincible. Today, I have a nice wife, a nice family, a nice home, a nice career, and nice friends—a nice life. I have learned to be grateful.

Kit Welchlin

Education: B.S., speech communication; M.A., speech communication, Minnesota State University-Mankato

Work: Former C.E.O. Currently, professional speaker and real estate investor.

Book: *The World's Greatest Speakers: Insider Secrets on How to Engage and Move Your Audience to Action* by Maria Lynn Johnson

Quote: If you have a race horse, you need to run it. —Anonymous

More: www.welchlin.com

*First say to yourself what you would be,
then do what you have to do.*

EPICTETUS

What Running 100 Miles Taught Me About Trust

Scott Welle

"You're going back out there."

It was 6:38 p.m. on Saturday, June 7, and I had been running for over 12 hours—since 6:00 a.m. that morning, in the 100-mile Kettle Moraine Ultra Marathon.

But I had a *big* problem. I was only at mile 63—and was lucky to have made it that far.

Looking up, the hot sun still commanded the summer sky…and showed no signs of relenting anytime soon. I sat—slumped—down for only the second time all day on a nearby picnic bench.

The last 15-20 miles had, for lack of a better term, kicked my ass. I was hot, tired and dehydrated. *Everything* on my body hurt, including my socks. Dirt and blood had caked on my legs from falling down twice.

I looked, and felt, like a beaten, defeated man.

Life is filled with defining moments and this was the defining moment in Kettle Moraine. The course route takes runners 31.5 miles out on a winding grass and dirt trail to a turn-around point, where you promptly reverse directions and run 31.5 miles back to the exact same location from which you started.

In a race in which more than 50% of the competitors will give up before crossing the finish line, this is the point where your ultra-marathon finishing dreams go to die.

I was already exhausted.

I was back at my car, which I was begging to take me to my hotel, the hot tub, the cold beer and my comfortable bed.

And with 37 daunting, unfinished miles left in the race, I was keenly aware that I was nowhere near done. The finish line may as well have been on another planet. It felt *that* far away.

As I sat on the picnic bench, I slowly lifted my head from my hands and turned to Diane and Missy, two of my good friends who had agreed to be my "crew" for the race and said, "I'm done. I've had enough."

They looked at me, paused slightly, and replied, "No, you're not."

I was not in the mood for a debate.

"Maybe you didn't hear me—I'm D.O.N.E.!," I shot back. "I've already run 63 miles, which is farther than I've ever run in my life! I have nothing more to prove. Nothing left in my tank."

Impressively, they stood their ground.

"Scott, you've got this! You came here to finish a race and that's what you're going to do. You'll never forgive us if we don't make you try. You're going back out there!"

In every speech I give, I advocate surrounding yourself with great, trusting people if you want to Outperform. And a criterion that determines whether someone falls into this category is if they'll tell you not just what you *want* to hear, but what you *need* to hear.

At that moment of the 100-mile Kettle Moraine Ultra Marathon, I so badly *wanted* to hear that it was okay to give up;

that I was validated in my decision to quit. Instead, I received a harsh dose of what I *needed* to hear; that I was selling myself short and was capable of doing more than I thought possible.

We *all* need these people in our lives. When I look at any accomplishment (personally, professionally, athletically) in my life that I would consider "significant" or "valuable," not a single one happened without being surrounded by other Outperformers.

It is *because of them* that I succeed.

I always say races, like life, are roller coasters, not train rides, and after I was lifted up from the picnic table and pushed to continue on, I had some of my best miles in the race. Don't get me wrong; there was no part of the last 37 miles that felt *easy*…but it did become more manageable, and I gained confidence with each passing mile. I ended up finishing the race in 21 hours and 6 minutes, taking 14th place in my first (and, likely, *only!*) ultra marathon.

I can honestly say that, if it wasn't for Missy and Diane, I wouldn't be a 100-mile runner. I would have given up. It took people believing in me at a time when I didn't believe in myself. That's what I think we were put here to do—to pull others up when they need it most. I'll always be thankful for the people who have helped me do that.

Believe you can and you're halfway there.
ANONYMOUS

Scott Welle

Education: B.A., psychology, University of Wisconsin-Madison; M.S., sport psychology, Georgia Southern University

Work: Entrepreneur and Chief Outperforming Officer (COO) of Outperform The Norm, 2015-present.

Book(s): *High Performance Habits* by Brendon Burchard and *Relentless* by Tim Grover

Quote: It is not the critic who counts; not the man who points out how the strong man stumbles, or where the doer of deeds could have done them better. The credit belongs to the man who is actually in the arena, whose face is marred by dust and sweat and blood; who strives valiantly; who errs, who comes short again and again, because there is no effort without error and shortcoming; but who does actually strive to do the deeds; who knows great enthusiasms, the great devotions; who spends himself in a worthy cause; who at the best knows in the end the triumph of high achievement, and who at the worst, if he fails, at least fails while daring greatly, so that his place shall never be with those cold and timid souls who neither know victory nor defeat. —Theodore Roosevelt—a passage from a 1910 speech referred to as "The Man in the Arena."

More:- ScottWelle.com, OutperformTheNorm.com
All social media channels are @scottwelle

What the World Gains from Optimism

Emily Parker

This June I will be graduating from high school. As I enter the next stage of my life, there are many unknowns about what the future holds. But that is the case at any stage of life. As I sit here, writing this and facing those unknowns, I can gaze down the path of my future with peace amidst the uncertainty.

The next several paragraphs are a speech that I gave for the 2017 Optimist International Oratorical Contest on the assigned topic "What the World Gains from Optimism." However, before I get there, I would like to share with you where I find optimism and hope for my own life.

As a Christian, I know that my Savior gave His life for me and loves me unconditionally and that one day I will see Him face to face. The joy and the certainty I have in this are what give me the ability to face my future regardless of what it holds. Without Christ, I can do nothing, but with Him, I can do whatever He gives me to do, no matter how difficult it may be. This is my source of hope and optimism. It is what empowers me to strive to be the best I can be to glorify my Savior.

This world is full of trials. We experience the pain of war, sickness, and heartache. Nevertheless, in the face of it all, an optimistic outlook has much to offer the world. Susan Boe, author of *Total Health: Choices for a Winning Lifestyle*, describes an optimist as "one who has the tendency to look on the more favorable side...to see the worst in complete realism, but still believe in the best." Let us consider some of the benefits that arise from optimism. First, optimism gives the world scientific and technological progress. Second, it provides the world with a happier and healthier population. Third, optimism brings the world more peace. Let us examine these benefits one at a time in more detail.

First, the world gains scientific and technological progress from optimism. For example, consider the inventions and the discoveries of Isaac Newton and Benjamin Franklin. In addition, Johannes Gutenberg influenced the printing industry with his movable-type printing press, George Washington Carver revolutionized agriculture with his techniques and research, and Sir Timothy Berners-Lee created the World Wide Web. Moreover, think about the compass, the telescope, the microscope, and the internal-combustion engine. Consider the airplane, the computer, space missions, and the advances in cancer treatment. Even a small degree of optimism, a willingness to press on, was an important factor to these scientific and technological innovations.

Second, the world gains a happier and healthier population from optimism. Many students have felt the pressure of homework assignments weigh heavily on their minds. I know I have. Many adults have experienced the stress of filing taxes and making ends meet. These are real issues, but fretting over them does not help. Again, Susan Boe in *Total Health* writes, "When distress occurs, the results of the stress...can be unhealthy and even fatal." Choosing to be optimistic, therefore, protects us from unnecessary illness. If we are optimistic, we are inclined to enjoy life more and can work without the stormy cloud of pessimism hanging over our heads. Furthermore, optimism helps us to act with kindness toward others, removing strain from our relationships. Overall, this gives the world a happier and healthier population.

Third, the world gains more peace from optimism. As optimistic people interact with others, optimism spreads from person to person. It is contagious! Lifting others up prepares and inspires them to help others. A world in which people encourage one another is a world of joy and peace. Personally, I have enjoyed volunteering for Feed My Starving Children, an organization that sends desperately needed food to countries around the world such as Kenya, Haiti, Iraq, and Ukraine. I have also loved packing gifts for Operation Christmas Child to send to children in more than 100 countries. Imagine a child who opens his gift to find his very first Matchbox car or a little girl who is clutching her new set of crayons and a coloring book. Both of these organizations provide children with reasons to feel loved and hopeful. When we are willing to give our time and resources to help and encourage others, we spread peace and joy throughout the world.

In conclusion, the world gains many benefits from optimism. Optimism creates the ideal environment for innovation, and it gives the world a happier and healthier population. Finally, optimism brings peace to the world. In the Public Broadcasting Service documentary *Never Stop Singing*, conductor Helmuth Rilling told of a memorable experience in Israel when his choir was performing with the Israel Philharmonic Orchestra. The Israeli national anthem was one of the pieces the orchestra was to play. As the choir stood and beautifully sang the anthem, the orchestra members stopped playing and broke out in tears. The choir was German, and they were singing the Israeli national anthem in Hebrew. These two ethnic groups had come together regardless of their past, and they were experiencing what can happen when we are willing to move forward. What a reason to be optimistic! God has blessed us with the gift of optimism, and we should use it because the world gains peace, hope, and healing.

Emily Parker

Education: 2018 graduate of Heritage Grace Academy Home School with plans to pursue a business degree and a piano minor in college

2017 Optimist International Oratorical Contest: 1st place in the Dakotas-Manitoba-Minnesota District of Optimist International

Book: *Seeking Allah, Finding Jesus* by Nabeel Qureshi

Quote: Courage is not simply one of the virtues but the form of every virtue at the testing point, which means at the point of highest reality —C. S. Lewis

The day is always his who works in it
with serenity and great aims.
RALPH W. EMERSON

Members

Terra Rathai, avantgardenstudio.com

I live in possibility.

EMILY DICKINSON

MEMBERS

Patrick Antonen
Dave Bartholomay
Kyle Bartholomay
Bob Brown
Bob Burmeister
Jeff Dahlman
Steve Dehler
Bill Dircks
Barb Einan
Mike Ericson
James Falvey
Bill Farmer
Sue Filbin
Doug Fischer
Ann Marie Forshay
Bob Freytag
Allen Gerdin
Gary Havir
Jon Heyer
Joel Huser
Craig Johnson
Peggy Johnson
Michelle Julius
Nora Keenan

Dick Klick
Jim Knuckey
Stephen Manweiler
David McKnight
Nancy Meyer
Patrick Miller
Steve Morris
Mark Nagel
Ralph Olsen
Scott Plum
Dan Prosser
Ted Risdall
Patty Sagert
Mark Smith
Curt Stockford
David Swan
Loren Swanson
Scott Thomas
Roger Williams
Ben Withhart
Warren Wolfe
Roger Worner
Mary Kay Ziniewicz

Just Show Up

Patrick Antonen

While I was completing my doctoral work in public administration at the University of South Dakota (USD), I was a teaching assistant who discovered that students who show up every day have a better academic experience. Since I had completed my undergraduate degree at the University of Minnesota, I would describe my experience as lackluster or average at best. However, once I began the Master in Public Administration (M.P.A.) program at USD, I learned that it was important to do the little things like attending class and participating in class every day. I learned to place a high priority on getting things done well in advance of their due date and preparing my weekly reading in advance of classes. I learned that it was important to spend time with my professors. I regularly attended office hours and met with my professors to better understand what they were looking for on exams and papers. I made it a point to visit Dakota Hall at USD, where all of the public administration professors were housed, at least twice a week to just show up and say hello. This meeting time allowed me an unusual insight into my professors' philosophy as it related to their course of study and their personal take on things.

In the second year of my M.P.A. program, I was granted a graduate assistantship which basically covered most of my college expenses. Since there were only two assistantships offered, I credit my success to being one of the few graduate students who had a personal relationship with all the faculty of the department. I always volunteered for events if the department needed assistance. I was an active member of the student association for public administration and served as president. That opportunity propelled me to a graduate fellowship with the South Dakota governor's office. I believe that all these positions were granted to me because I showed up to my professors and colleagues.

When I served as an adjunct instructor for the University of South Dakota and Des Moines Area Community College, I observed that students who attended every class, and more importantly would attend office hours, generally had better grades. Managing your time and resisting the temptation of the excessive extracurricular activities of college life are the keys to being successful in your undergraduate and graduate programs. Not only did my chronological age play a factor, but also cohesive academic experience at USD allowed me to flourish in my chosen professional area. I have surprised many of my friends when I say that I completed my M.P.A. degree as well as classwork and the comprehensive exam for fulfillment of my Doctor of Philosophy in Public Administration (Ph.D.). My story is not complete in that I am writing now my dissertation, with each week a little closer to having it completed. Life sometimes gets in the way, but if you keep showing up, you will succeed in your life's endeavors.

Patrick Antonen

Education: B.S., sociology of law, University of Minnesota; masters of public administration, University of South Dakota; Ph.D. public administration, currently ABD, University of South Dakota

Work: City Administrator, Circle Pines, Minnesota, since 2016; city administrator, Centerville, Iowa, three years; project officer, Department of Public Safety for State of Iowa, two years; graduate assistant/lecturer, University of South Dakota, two years; doctoral fellowship, South Dakota governor's office, 2008–2009.

Book: *Good to Great* by Jim Collins

Quote: Never give in. Never give in. Never, never, never, never—in nothing, great or small, large or petty—never give in, except to convictions of honour and good sense. Never yield to force. Never yield to the apparently overwhelming might of the enemy. —Winston Churchill 10/29/1941

Is an Optimist a Fool?

Dave Bartholomay

Take a look around. There is a seemingly endless run of stories in the news about the bad shape of our world. Nasty partisan gridlock in St. Paul and in Washington, D.C. Rich getting richer and poor getting poorer. Church attendance is down, anger and hate seem to be up, good jobs gone overseas, distrust of our institutions, and a loss of hope for too many of our citizens. And in the midst of all that and more bad news, I am an optimist. Does that make me a fool?

I know a woman from my church who is really struggling. She is fighting a nasty cancer that wants to take her away from her wonderful and loving husband and two teenage boys. Should she just give up? Is it a mistake for her to be optimistic and believe she can beat this disease?

I know a lot of Centennial High School teachers who are helping kids in their classrooms who are facing difficult life situations. These teachers and staff work very hard to help kids who, in all likelihood, are going to have a very tough time being "successful" in modern-day America. But they push on day by day, trying again and again to find ways to educate and inspire these kids to beat the odds; to be optimistic about their future. Are they really going to make a difference? Should they just give up and stop caring?

I know a big-city mayor, long retired, who was a fountain of hope and new ideas when he was in office. The other day he confided that, in his old age, as he has seen losses and setbacks, he has become more and more pessimistic about life. Given all he has seen, would he be a fool to be optimistic about the future?

No, absolutely not!

Being an "optimist" with a positive attitude on life is not about being happy when things are going good and viewed as "out of touch" when things are going rough. An optimist understands that there will be failures; we don't live in a fantasy land. But we learn from our failures and we believe that success will inevitably follow those failures.

I recently joined the newly formed Roseville Area Optimist Club that serves the north-metro area. Part of their mission is to work each day to make the future brighter by bringing out the best in children, in their communities, and in themselves. I sometimes jokingly refer to the Optimist Club as a "support group" for when I don't feel quite so positive about the future. I'm also a member of an Optimist book club with my friend, former Centennial superintendent Roger Worner. The books we read are so inspiring and the people we meet so wonderful that the monthly meetings can't come soon enough.

So why am I telling you all of this? Because I don't think being optimistic is foolish. In fact, I think it is the only way to a happy, successful, and fulfilling life. I imagine a world in which we see the positive in situations; where we have hope in resolving tough problems—a world where our focus on maintaining a positive attitude shapes the way we see our world and thus increases the possibilities for improving our families and our communities. I imagine a world in which people treating people kindly and with care inspires our youth to take that lesson into a bright future.

Please take a minute and, as the old saying goes, "count your blessings." There are more than you think, and with an optimistic approach to life, you can find many more.

Dave Bartholomay

Education: B.S. and M.A., political science, Arizona State University

Work: Office of Collaboration and Dispute Resolution, State of Minnesota, program coordinator, one year; Mayor of Circle Pines.

Book: *Man's Search for Meaning* by Viktor Frankl

Quote: God doesn't need your good works, but your neighbor does. —Martin Luther

More: www.davebartholomay.com

Optimism is the faith that leads to achievement.
Nothing can be done without hope and confidence.

HELEN KELLER

Backpacking With Optimism

Kyle Bartholomay

Most people would be worried about traveling, backpacking around Europe by themselves, especially after finishing college. I, however, was not worried. I have been fortunate enough to go to our Optimist Club meetings for the past six months and optimism was one of the many things I packed in my 50-pound backpack around Europe.

It was very helpful to hear from all the people who helped prepare me for my journey by sharing experiences and tips. The people who cared about me most were warning me of all the possible dangers and problems I could run into.

After listening to the advice, I had two choices when making decisions on the trip:

1. Bring an optimistic attitude

2. Bring a pessimistic attitude

I decided to bring an optimistic attitude on my journey. What this meant for me was I could either start a conversation with someone from Germany or Switzerland, or I could keep to myself. I could stay in during the night due to the fear of being pick-pocketed, or I could go out and have fun. I could stay away and not interact with the locals, or I could learn about a different culture from people who are different from me.

Talking to strangers is usually not advised, starting at a young age, but I never ran into an individual who didn't want to help me and hear my story of traveling. I decided that I would take an optimistic approach about these dangers and be aware of my surroundings to make the most of my experience.

I understand many of the events on my trip could have gone terribly wrong, but I tried to see the light in every situation instead of the dark things that could happen. My outlook gave me an opportunity to feel stress-free and have an unforgettable trip.

If there is one piece of advice I wish everyone knew before going on their next adventure, it would be:

Don't forget to pack optimism on your next trip.

Kyle Bartholomay

Education: B.S., finance and marketing, Concordia College, Moorhead, MN

Work: Brokerage associate, U.S. Bancorp.

Book: *Start With Why* by Simon Sinek

Quote: What lies behind us and what lies ahead of us are tiny matters compared to what lives within us. —Henry David Thoreau

Poverty is a State of Mind

Bob Brown

The statement "Poverty is a state of mind" has been challenged by many people, but I think, based on my life experience, there is a lot of truth in it.

My dad's parents emigrated from New Brunswick, Canada, and settled in Stillwater as the lumber industry moved to the Midwest in the late 19th century. My mom's parents were Italian immigrants who settled in St. Paul. Both families struggled to survive. Both of my parents were uneducated according to the standards of today. My dad dropped out of school in the fourth grade to help his mother at home when she was ill. With both her parents speaking only Italian, my mother went to school to learn English and ultimately completed the 8th grade.

Because of the wound he received as a Marine in World War I, and the onset of the depression which limited work opportunities, my dad was unemployed much of the time as I was growing up, but he did get a small pension as a disabled veteran. My mother worked in low-paying retail jobs, but she somehow managed to save a little and make a weekly contribution to church.

Our large family (six kids, with my oldest sister being 18 years older than I) was pretty crowded in my gramma's house until my mother borrowed $100 from her sister in 1940 to make a down payment on a house costing $900. We were excited to have a house of our own even though there was no central heat and no plumbing or running water, and only two bedrooms for my parents and the four of us kids still living at home.

While the food was simple, we always had enough to eat. Even though we were in the city of Stillwater, we raised chickens in the backyard and had a garden with strawberries and vegetables.

When my brother, Dick, went in the Navy after graduating from high school, all of my brothers were in the service during World War II. At about the same time, my dad, despite his physical limitations, was hired by the post office due to the shortage of men because most of the younger men were in the service. This meant my dad now had a regular income. I was lucky being the youngest member of the family at a time when we had a regular income.

Several years later, when my brother Dick wrote a book, one of the reviewers wrote that he was raised in abject poverty. *We never considered ourselves poor; we just didn't have any money.* What we did have was love and support from our family and friends. My mother taught us strong religious values and the importance of hard work. Due to his disability, my dad was home most of the time and he taught us the importance of reading for knowledge and being tolerant of people who had a difference of opinions. From the time I was little he would talk to me as if I were an adult, never talking down to me and also allowing me to disagree with him. I learned more from my parents than from all my college professors combined.

What I see today is a poverty of respect for others and their opinions, a poverty of knowledge about how the government should work, and a poverty of commitment to help people when they need help. Money alone cannot solve those problems.

Education: Ph.D., educational leadership, University of Minnesota

Work: Professor emeritus of educational leadership, policy and administration at the University of St. Thomas and former Republican Minnesota state senator.

Book: *Broken Bonds: What Family Fragmentation Means for America's Future* by Mitch Pearlstein

Quote: A leader is best when people barely know he exists, when his work is done, his aim fulfilled, they will say: "We did it ourselves." —Lao Tzu

There is no duty we so underrate as the duty of being happy.
ROBERT LOUIS STEVENSON

The One-percent Difference

Bob Burmeister

It was almost 5:30 p.m. on New Year's Eve 1977 when the call came that my father was being rushed into surgery. My mother was here in Minnesota visiting for the Christmas holidays, but my dad had stayed in Milwaukee as his aged mother was in the hospital with pneumonia. Now he, too, was in the same hospital in the middle of what amounted to a 10-inch snowfall.

A surgical team had to be called in to repair a two-and-one-half-inch tear in an aneurysm of the renal artery. While my father received twenty-two units of blood and nine units of plasma during the operation, and he survived the night, his prospects were grim and his condition was critical.

We had gathered with our faith community for a New Year's Eve dinner and midnight service to enter the New Year, which suddenly had become very tenuous. Being as we were physically distant and had no communication during the surgery, our primary recourse was to pray and to ask the gathered assembly to join us in that effort.

Attempts the following day to get my mother on a plane were futile. She made it to the gate, with us with her, in the days when you could accompany passengers to their planes, only to find out that all flights had been canceled due to the snowstorm in Milwaukee. So instead, my wife and I packed up the car and left to drive the next day with a three-year-old, a five-month-old and my mother all protesting loudly in the back seat.

We arrived at the hospital eight hours later as the roads were still snow covered and hazardous. As we met the doctor in my father's intensive-care room, he declared, "Your father has a 50/50 chance to survive." My response was immediate. "With all due respect, doctor, my father has a 51/49 percent chance to live because people of faith have been and are praying for him!"

It was a one-percent difference, but within it was contained faith, hope and love.

The road that followed was not easy. Dad was transferred to Milwaukee County General Hospital from our local suburban hospital since he needed dialysis. He spent 37 days in the hospital, but when he got home, he was a changed man. His stoic German nature was transformed into a warmer, more approachable person.

Dad lived for 13 additional years, from age 67 to 80, and even spent some of that time volunteering as a "red coat" in the very hospital where the surgery had been performed. His mother had recovered, too, and he continued to care for her until she died at the age of 96.

Later we learned that statistically, the survival rate of an event such as my dad's is 5% at best.

But it was the one percent that made the difference between life and death!

Bob Burmeister

Education: B.A., St. Olaf College (Global Semester III); M.Div., Luther Theological Seminary

Work: Associate pastor, North Heights Lutheran Church for 41 years.

Book: The *Bible,* as it still contains the words of LIFE!

Quote: All the days ordained for me were written in your book before one of them came to be. —Psalm 139:16

More: www.nhlc.org

The boldest and most ridiculous hope has sometimes been the cause of extraordinary success.
LUC DE CLAPIERS, MARQUIS DE VAUVENARGUES

Mission Statement

Jeff Dahlman

I was once asked to write a mission statement. This was a mission statement intended not for a company or organization, but for myself. My first thought was simple…what *is* a mission statement?

While many definitions exist, they are very similar in dialogue. Essentially, a mission statement is **a formal summary of the aims and values of a company, organization, or individual.** Search any major company on the internet, and you will typically find their mission statement on their home page. For any business, the mission statement is their end goal; everything they do should focus and revolve around the sustainability, growth, and success of the mission.

A mission statement should not be long and overly-detailed. It should represent your values and be an expression of your desires and intent. I recommend researching examples of mission statements, but to also be original. Be honest with yourself. Your mission should only be shared with others if you feel compelled to do so. If you feel your mission changes with time, adjust accordingly. What you feel now may completely change in the future, and that is the wonderful part of a mission statement…it can change with you.

After considerable thought, my mission quickly materialized. I want to see those around me happy and successful, and I can help that by doing everything I can to be a better person for everyone.

My mission statement: To be the best possible version of myself for those around me, so that they may become the best possible version of who they want to be.

Again, I encourage you to be honest with yourself when writing your statement. It should reflect who you are, and what you intend to do!

Jeff Dahlman

Education: B.A., secondary education, University of Minnesota-Duluth

Work: Executive director, Twin Cities Kids In Need Resource Center, since September 2016.

Book: *The Art of Racing in the Rain* by Garth Stein

Quote: If the path be beautiful, let us not ask where it leads.
—Anatole France

More: jeffd@kinf.org | www.tckinrc.org | www.kinf.org
@TCKidsInNeed

Optimism in a Small Town

Steve Dehler

"Who are you riding with?" my mother asked, as the last items were being loaded. "I'm going to ride in the truck with Uncle Anthony and Ellen," I squealed. When you're five years old and your parents tell you that we're moving to a new house, you don't really ask questions! It's kind of like the beginning of a new adventure. For me that adventure started in March 1956. I don't remember the hour-long ride; I could barely see over the dashboard. I do remember, though, that we stopped finally in a small alley and the house was on the right-hand side. I was sitting between my sister Ellen and Uncle Anthony. There was a big snow drift along the side of the road. Ellen got out first on the right-hand side and slipped and fell right into the snow. I got out carefully then and jumped into the snow, wiped myself off, and ran into the house.

Many thoughts go through five-year-olds' minds when they move into a new house like, "When are we going to eat?" and "Where are we going to sleep?" That didn't really resonate in my mind. I was just excited about seeing all the furniture that had been left in the house and new places to explore. I wasn't really looking toward making new friends because we really only had each other on the farm and we never really had many friends—just each other and some relatives who showed up once in a while.

My name is Steve Dehler and I come from a family of nine children. This was the first time we had a house in a city. Prior to that, we lived on three farms within a period of five years. Thinking back on that time, I think we were all filled with optimism. Dad was working in St. Cloud. We have a new house in St. Joseph, and everybody seemed happy! Optimistic, I'm sure! Having not ever heard the word optimism at age five, I can only imagine that optimism is what I felt. I was just like most kids in those days. We walked to school in the morning, came home for lunch, went back to school after an hour and studied in school until 4 o'clock. We met neighborhood kids and played a lot of outside games. We were hardly ever in the house. A lot of "Hide and Seek." We called it, " I Will Draw the Frying Pan, Who Will Poke the Wiener In." When you're finished laughing at that name, I'll just say, it was quite a fun game.

I don't remember, today, that I thought a lot about what I was going to do when I grew up. I figured that was just going to happen. I knew I would be something when I grew up so when I was 12 years old, I had an opportunity to work for my uncle in North Dakota on a farm. I jumped at the chance that maybe I'm going to be a farmer! Nope, not a farmer, even though I spent the next two summers working on farms.

One day, after that first summer on the farm, my life changed. I was upstairs, during the evening, in my room with my brother, Leo. We were both lying in our own beds reading when my Dad hollers up the stairway, "Hey, Mr. Linnemann is looking for someone to help him up at the store if you guys are interested!" My brother didn't say a word. He is older than I am so I said to Dad that I would go see Mr. Linnemann. At least it would get me out of the house doing something!

After working on that farm from five in the morning until 10 at night for the last three months, I was kind of anxious to not just sit around. I still did not know what I was going to be when I grew up but I figured somehow it would be revealed to me. Maybe this is it. I'll be a grocer! Anyway, it wouldn't hurt to check it out.

I went to town and met Mr. HP Linnemann! He showed me the fluorescent light bulbs that needed washing. That was my first job at age 13 in Linnemann's Store. I worked until I was 20 and then was hired as the manager. At 21, I married the boss's daughter, Jean, and at 31, my wife and I bought the business and worked it together until I was 41. Not wanting to go bankrupt, we then just closed the business. It was a small Ma and Pa store started by the Linnemann family in 1855. When I started working, they had sales of about $50,000 a year and throughout my career I felt each day that tomorrow we could turn that corner! We could go from a survival mode to finally making a profit! When I first started, I really didn't think that I would make this my career—that I would be a grocer when I grew up—but the more I got involved with the business of helping people and with helping the Linnemann family with their store, the more I felt that this was the career path I was supposed to be taking!

After getting married, I was certainly involved with the family business! Each day, I would think of different ways that we could improve the displays or improve our products so that people would want to shop at Linnemann's instead of our competition 20 feet away or in St. Cloud, only seven miles away. There was always something I could do to get me closer to that corner I was aiming for. I was optimistic, so every positive change that we made was to just get around that corner so I could see light.

One can't only work, so I did get involved in things that went on in our community.

I remember, while working in the store one day, Dennis Stueve, a local car mechanic, stopped in and encouraged me to go to a meeting at the La Playette. The St. Cloud Jaycees wanted to extend a chapter here in St. Joseph. I remember telling Dennis that I really did not have time to go to meetings because of all the work there was at the store. I then thought about it more, and I was curious. I felt I should not only be working in the store! Maybe getting involved in some community activities would benefit the business.

I showed up at the meeting, asked some questions, and by the end of that meeting, I was elected the charter president! By the way, did I tell you yet, I am a very shy person but I accepted the nomination and the challenge to help me get rid of that shyness. To me, each time something happened in my life, I always figured it was a sign that maybe this would help me discover what I am to be when I grow up! I was 22 and was optimistic that my future lay ahead, and that someday I would discover what my life's journey would hold for me.

During that first year and a half as the charter president, I got over the fear of standing in front of a group of people and learned how to be a leader! Following that "training," I was asked to be on my church's parish council and when I said yes, I was elected to a four-year term. During those first two formative years of setting a parish budget and seeing how decisions on the city council were affecting my business, my world was getting larger! I remember complaining to my mother about something that was happening in St. Joseph. I don't remember what it was but I remember what she said! "Why are you complaining to me? Why don't you go out and do something about it?" So contrary to a lot of advice I got from different people in the community, I decided to run for mayor! Since no one was signing up, I thought this was my calling. Maybe I can be a grocer and be involved in local government.

Within a day following my application to be on the ballot, eight other people signed up even though it was the last day to sign up. It looked like I inspired some activity! I was optimistic! I knew a lot of people, but at age 23, I ended up losing to all eight, including a character who was inebriated most of the time!

I saw the light and decided to attend the city council meetings and become familiar with their activities before filing again. After two years of attending council meetings, I ran again for city council and got elected. I decided to run for city council instead of mayor. I wanted to learn how to be a winner, so in 1975 at the age of 25, I began a career of community service through elected public office.

Following 16 years of being on the city council and then two years as mayor, an opportunity came up so I ran for and was elected to the Minnesota House of Representatives! Still wondering what I was going to be when I grew up, I knew that something in my life was going to tell me when we closed the store in June 1991. I was ready to try something different, and three part-time jobs were not very much fun to juggle.

A spot opened up locally for a legislative position so again I thought, why not? Why not try? I didn't really only want to try, though, but win! I worked hard to get elected. Maybe this was going to be my career when I grew up? Ten years and five elections later, redistricting put me into my colleague's legislative area and circumstances in my life didn't allow me to continue, so not wanting to go back into the grocery business,

I got a job at Sears to see how large corporations work. Maybe this was what I was supposed to be—a department manager in the "softer side of Sears"! I gave it a try! After four years of working in corporate retail and financially starving, I sought out and was able to get a job as a detention deputy for the Hennepin County jail. I was 57 now and wasn't sure what I was going to be when I grew up. Maybe this was it—a jailer! "Jailer Dehler." I should have known!

I retired last April following 10 years as a detention deputy. I had the opportunity to look back at my life and I have finally realized what it was that I was supposed to be when I grew up! Do you know what? I was that person all my life! My optimism knew that life would send me around that corner, and around each corner there was someone who needed my help! I was where I belonged, in every facet of my customer-service career! I was a servant to strangers, my family, and to my friends, and I can't imagine a better life!

One event, above all others, stands out while working at Linnemann's. One evening, we were relatively busy and a man came in who was dressed somewhat disheveled. He asked for some pipe tobacco and asked to charge it. I just handed him the tobacco and a smile and told him he could just have it. The man thanked me and left. The next customer—who was new to the St. Joseph community—asked me why I had given the man the tobacco. I told her, without giving it a second thought, "You never know what Jesus will look like when he returns, and I figured I was just being tested!"

In the customer-service world, you are constantly being tested!
—*Thank God for Optimism!*

Steve Dehler

Education: Accounting and economics, College of St. Benedict and St. John's University

Work: Retail grocer, Sears, corrections officer, dispatcher, mayor and city council member, St. Joseph, MN; Minnesota House of Representatives.

Book: *Anastasia* by Vladimir Megre

Quote: Quality remains long after the price is forgotten —Author unknown! —*I learned this saying during my early days at Linnemann's Store in St. Joseph, Minnesota*

More: SteveDehler.com

*Show yourself more human than critical
and your pleasure will increase.*

DOMENICO SCARLATTI

A Lifetime of Todays

Steve Dehler

A lifetime of todays is what we have within.

Each moment gives us the opportunity to give the world a spin.

We're not given much to start except family and friends who show us the way,

So it's up to us to do our part to fill each moment of every day

With love, laughter, and letting go,
with dreams and courage and seeds to sow.

So when I go to bed each night, I'm thankful for what came my way,

And grateful for a lifetime of todays!

A Journey from
Pessimism to Optimism

Bill Dircks

I grew up as a painfully shy person and that shyness caused me to be negative and pessimistic more often than not. I had no real reason to be negative or pessimistic. I grew up in a stable family in the suburbs. I was a good student and participated in numerous sports and other activities. Once I got to know someone, I was a different person around them compared to people I didn't know. I was much more personable and talkative.

After I graduated from the University of Minnesota, I took a job somewhat related to my finance major but it also included some sales and that was extremely difficult for me. I could not get myself to talk to potential clients and I failed miserably. Following that experience, I went back to something I discovered I loved, which was public works. I had been a seasonal employee for a few years at three different cities and really enjoyed the work, so I decided to give it a shot full time.

I started for the City of Little Canada and quickly learned that it can be a very pessimistic profession. Things seem to always go wrong. It seemed a rare occurrence that a project would go smoothly. It is also easy to get caught up in the negative comments from residents and contractors.

I found my way and enjoyed what I was doing and then was promoted to superintendent. It became even easier to be pessimistic because now I had to field the angry calls and emails directly. It would have been easy to let it get me down and join the chorus of negativity and pessimism, but I decided to approach things differently. I decided I was going to be as positive as I could and set an example for my crew and all city staff. I became more optimistic and charged ahead, and it has been a revelation.

I found that people just want to talk to someone, and if you listen to them and give them time, they appreciate what you do and come around to a more positive side. There are always going to be some folks who never will accept anything and want to argue, but for the most part, my experiences with people have been filled with wins. I do everything I can to help people. I try not to say "no" to anything and look for a solution that will work for everyone involved. Going the extra mile for people gives me a positive charge and helps keep my spirits up during the more negative times.

I joined the Roseville Area Optimist Club as soon it was formed and have seen my optimism soar even more. It is a wonderful experience to get together once a month and talk to positive people and hear their own stories of optimism, positivity, and success. I am now a public works director and I am excited for my future as I optimistically plow ahead in my career and in my personal life.

Bill Dircks

Education: B.S., finance, Carlson School of Management-University of Minnesota

Professional: Public works director, City of Little Canada, 2005-present; public works maintenance, City of Little Canada, 2001-2005.

Book: *Primal Leadership by* Daniel Goleman

Quote: Choose to be optimistic, it feels better. —Dalai Lama XIV

Everything's gonna be alright.
BOB MARLEY

The Love of a Family
is Life's Greatest Blessing

Barb Einan

I've been optimistic my whole life. In fact, I was a cheerleader in both high school and four years of college. I was president of a pep club of 250+ members at St. Paul Central High School.

A girl who was getting into the real estate business in 1985 said to me recently that the manager of her office said she should talk to Barb Einan and see if she had any advice for you. She said I told her to surround herself with positive people and if you're on the Tuesday tour bus and end up sitting next to someone negative, move and sit next to someone positive.

When Don Salverda asked me to meet with him and Terry Gorman, who is the District Governor of Optimist International, about starting a Roseville Optimist Club, I said I'm totally in!!! Thus, I am a founding member of the club, and now I'm in two optimist book clubs and one book club for the Roseville Rotary. I look forward every month to spending time with my new optimist friends at our meetings. Both the speakers and the members are amazing.

Well, my story is about the men in my life, starting with my dad, Ed Peterson. He gave me the greatest gift anyone could give to another person. He believed in me. I read recently that a girl gets her self-esteem from her dad. Your dad is your first hero. If something was broken, he could fix it. If I was sad, he made me smile. If I was scared, he made me feel safe. If my self-confidence was shaken, he built it back up. If I needed to know I was loved, he came through with flying colors. He was my first hero, and I'll never stop believing in him or being grateful he was my dad. One of the quotes I love is the definition of success: "You can use any measure when you're speaking of success, you can measure it in a fancy home, expensive car, or dress, but the measure of real success—the one you cannot spend—it's the way your kids describe you when talking to a friend."

The next man in my life who was so special to me was my older brother "Eddie." He was five years older than I was and I absolutely adored him. He was president of his confirmation class, a jet pilot, and a lieutenant in the Air Force. However, he was tragically killed at age 22 on his motorcycle on his way to Macalester College when a food truck made an illegal turn in front of him at Como and Snelling. Eddie's plan was to get his college degree and then fly for Northwest Airlines. He was my parents' first child and only son.

The third important man in my life is Dick Einan, the man I dated at Macalester during my junior and senior years and then married right after college. My dad was my role model when I picked my husband. This was the best decision of my life! After 25 years with the Federal Reserve Bank of Minneapolis and his job as community affairs officer, Dick joined me in real estate sales and we became "Spouses Selling Houses."

After teaching for four years, Dick and I started our family which produced the fourth important man in my life, our son Kent Richard Einan. So, there is this boy. He kind of stole my heart; he calls me Mom! Nothing makes a parent happier than to see their son has become a great father with the *strength* to take care of others, the *understanding* to handle the challenges and the opportunities in life, and the *love* to make his family happy.

Our family was completed with a wonderful daughter, Kimberly Jill Einan, and we have five amazing grandchildren: Lindy, Lauren, and Kyle Einan and Jake and Madison Stratton.

Happiness isn't getting what you want all the time. It's about loving what you have and being grateful for it. When we wake up in the morning we "choose happy."

The life-lesson principles of gratitude

"Watch your thoughts; they become words. Watch your words; they become actions. Watch your actions; they become habits. Watch your habits; they become character. Watch your character; it becomes your destiny."

Barb Einan

Education: B.A., physical education, Macalester College

Work: Teacher, St. Paul Public Schools; assistant real estate training director; real estate agent, Edina Realty, Inc. Family team—Einan Home Team (Barb, Dick, and Kent); Chairman's and Master's Circle awards home-staging professional, Edina Realty; #1 in sales 18 years running.

Book: *Positive Words, Powerful Results* by Hal Urban

Quote: There is nothing more beautiful than someone who goes out of their way to make life more beautiful for others. —Mandy Hale

Smile, Life is a Journey

Mike Ericson

I am a runner.

I enjoy being a runner. I like that over the many miles I have run, each has given me the strength and hope to be a better person. I like to learn and I like to experience life. I remember the people and places I have been and the experiences that running has provided me. There are hundreds of memories etched in my mind, and the mental, physical, and spiritual challenges that I have faced helped to develop me into the person I am today.

I am a very positive person. I have always been like that. I like being around positive people. We have a synergy and energy about us. We have "can-do" attitudes and we get things done. I live every day to the highest, and share with my family a focus on family, friends, and faith. I am a proud charter member of the Roseville Area Optimist Club.

I am also a city government professional for more than 28 years, working in eight cities and a county. I have been blessed to work for more than 20 years as a city administrator in five cities. It has been an incredibly rewarding career. I'm currently working in Brooklyn Center. Before that, I worked for Centerville, Landfall, Maple Plain, Maplewood, Hugo, Maplewood, Watertown, St. Louis County, and Woodbury. In my teenage years, and later on in college, I actually worked for the Brooklyn Center Park and Recreation Department for 13 years, and it was so much fun. It is ironic I am back where I started so long ago, more than 40 years later.

Most people know me as the city administrator for the City of Hugo for more than eleven years beginning in 2000. Hugo changed almost overnight from a farming community, with dramatic increases in residential, commercial, and retail construction and a current population of 13,417. In 2010, Hugo was recognized by the *Minneapolis/St. Paul Business Journal* as the fastest-growing city during the past decade. In 2008, Hugo was hit by an F-3 tornado, causing significant damage to homes and businesses, and the loss of a little boy, Nate Prindle. I am so proud of the emergency-response efforts of the city and the resounding cleanup activities the Saturday afterward. This major-life experience was a "God Moment" to be sure. I was fortunate to receive excellent disaster training many years ago with a 90-person team from Ramsey County when we flew to Washington, D.C., to the National Disaster Preparedness Training Center.

I earned my Bachelor of Science degree in public administration from Winona State University in 1986, and served as president of the student senate during my senior year. I earned my graduate degree in urban and regional studies from Minnesota State University, Mankato, in 1990. I am a native of Brooklyn Park and graduated from Osseo High School. I grew up in a normal, middle-class family with an older brother, Steve, and three younger sisters—Sheri, Patti, and Joni. My dad, LeRoy, was a residential roofer and my mom, Millie, was a bookkeeper/office manager with Lathers Local #190-Minneapolis.

I became a commercial construction worker and card-carrying member of Lathers Local #190 and worked on many buildings in the Twin Cities. During a summer internship after college, I worked for a congressman in Washington, D.C., and later on as a construction worker on the Pentagon. Prior to that, I helped build the EPCOT Center in Orlando, Florida, and saved my money and went back to college and reinvented myself.

My wife, Suzanne, is a special-education teacher in Mahtomedi. We have three children: Rachel, Paige, and Westin. We have lived in Maplewood for the past nineteen years. I have served as president of both the Minnesota City/ County Management Association (MCMA) and Metropolitan Area Management Association (MAMA), and even served as the treasurer of MAUMA, the former state assistant's group now known as APMP.

I volunteer in Maplewood, ISD #622 schools, and at St. Mark's Lutheran Church. I am a volunteer board member of the Maplewood Historical Society. I am very active at my church as an usher, communion assistant, confirmation mentor, personnel committee member, 125 Capital Campaign member, and have been elected to the church council where I served as president more than 12 years ago. I was recently voted back on the council where I will serve a three-year term.

In addition, I enjoy coaching youth sports. I have coached for thirteen years in the Maplewood Sports League with all three of my children. Baseball, softball, soccer, and basketball have been the focus of my coaching. When I was younger, I was fortunate to coach the Aces Women's Softball Team to a State Class-B Championship. After three years as coach of the Park Center Pirates 9th-grade girls fast-pitch softball team, I will begin my fourth year as coach of the North St. Paul High 9th-grade girls fast-pitch softball team. I teach life lessons with the student athletes as well as fundamentals, friends, and fun.

I enjoy family camping, fishing, hunting, reading, writing, and running. Did I say I was a runner?

Mike Ericson

Education: B.S., public administration, Winona State University; M.A., urban and regional studies, Minnesota State University, Mankato

Work: City government for 28 years for eight cities and a county, and as a city administrator for more than 20 years in five cities. Currently work in community development for the City of Brooklyn Center.

Book: *Outperform the Norm* by Scott Welle

Quote: Some people see things as they are and say "Why?" I dream things that never were and say "Why not? "
—George Bernard Shaw

More: I am on Facebook, Linked In, and Twitter

Of all the gifts bestowed by nature on human beings, hearty laughter must be close to the top.
NORMAN COUSINS

What I Learned and What I Can Share With My New Friends at the Roseville Area Optimist Club

James Falvey

As a brand new member of the Roseville Area Optimist Club, I welcome an opportunity to share with my fellow members, even if I haven't had a chance to meet most of you in person just yet.

As someone who has chosen to take the long road in life, I am fortunate to have enjoyed a breadth of experiences that have taught me many valuable life lessons. One of those life lessons is the power of daydreaming.

Although I have a B.A. degree now, I initially dropped out of the University of Minnesota, Duluth, after my second year so that I could experience a little more life and make a more informed decision about my eventual career path.

While working odd jobs, I dreamt about being in a rock band, singing and making a statement. I had no credible reason to think that I could. I wasn't actually a singer; couldn't read or write music. But I could dream. And dream I did. I would go to bed at night just imagining what it would be like, how I would approach the opportunity, how I would present myself. It got to the point where the dream was almost enough by itself. I simply enjoyed thinking about it.

Well, while thinking about all of this, I found a friend who was a gifted guitar player who shared my dream. To make a long story short, a year later we were headlining a show at First Avenue's main stage after having won "battle of the bands" at the old Seventh Street Entry.

My dream came true!

I continued to work odd jobs to support myself. The band didn't make any significant money and we eventually broke up. One of the odd jobs I happened into was going door-to-door, fundraising for an international environmental organization.

As a lowly canvasser, working in an outpost office, I dreamed of becoming one of the elite environmental activists who got to go around conducting daredevil protests aimed at drawing attention to issues most people didn't think to care about. And although my chances of becoming a professional protester were incredibly close to zero, I dreamt long and hard about what it would be like. I envisioned myself in the rubber boat saving the whale, or up on the smokestack, hanging the banner and inspiring the world around me to do better by our fragile planet.

I had no credible reason to think that I could. I wasn't actually a mountain climber or sailor. But I could dream. And dream I did. I would go to bed at night just imagining what it would be like, how I would approach the opportunity, how I would present myself. It got to the point where the dream was almost enough by itself. I simply enjoyed thinking about it.

Well, while thinking about all of this, an opportunity to stage a protest here in the Twin Cities presented itself. To make a long story short, a year later I found myself as part of the nine-person North American Action Team, responsible for supporting protests and acts of civil disobedience throughout the United States and Canada.

My dream came true!

I was and still am an incredibly average person. If I have one advantage in life, it is the fact that I had parents who believed in me. They often told me that there wasn't anything in the world I couldn't do.

I might have been just dumb enough to believe them because that ingrained optimism—combined with having the time to dream, allowing myself to see possibilities, and having confidence that I, too, could achieve success—were all-important components of realizing those dreams.

James Falvey

Education: B.A., management of human service organizations Concordia University, Saint Paul; candidate for M.A., servant leadership, Viterbo University, La Crosse, WI

Work: Executive director, Little Brothers—Friends of the Elderly, Minneapolis/St. Paul Chapter. Past president, Great Rivers United Way (La Crosse, WI), former certified fundraising executive (CFRE) with 20 years' experience in leadership and fundraising in higher education, human service and environmental organizations.

Book: *The Perennial Philosophy* by Aldous Huxley

Quote: The first responsibility of a leader is to define reality. The last is to say thank you. In between, the leader is a servant. —Max DePree

Parting Gifts

Bill Farmer

My model of optimism is not one of perpetual bright sunshine. Rather, the model is one of rays of light periodically breaking through the overcast. The light teases us to see beyond all current opportunities for gloom; to be alert to moments of delight as they arrive, especially when least expected.

My mother had alzheimers for the last sixteen years of her life. During the first half of my mother's long, progressive decline, I was fully consumed by various life challenges. My siblings carried the load in ensuring my mother's comfort and care. My sister eventually moved Mom into a nursing home near her home and took upon herself the responsibility that Mom's decline into darkness would not be without a measure of dignity.

The challenges that I was dealing with at the time centered around my desire to start a family. I was back to college in my 30s, pretty broke, but full of hope. I was engaged to a Japanese woman, whom I had met while studying abroad. I was doing well in school. Rays of hope, moments of joy emerged from the day-to-day grind.

As a part of my sister's efforts to engage and stimulate Mom, she arranged a family reunion. The other three of Mom's kids converged on my sister's home from across the country, with families, or the beginnings of family, in tow.

My sister had adopted a Korean daughter; my brother had done the same. On the beautiful spring day of the family reunion, my two nieces hovered most of the day around my fiancée. They were clearly delighted to have an Asian adult ready to join the family.

I was sitting on the back deck at the reunion, next to my mom. We were on a bench in the shade, surveying all the activity going on in the four corners of the yard. It was enough to spark a conversation, normally, but not in these circumstances. Mom hadn't uttered a comprehensible word for over a year, and her cognitive ability appeared to have completely abandoned her.

I was rolling all that over gloomily in my mind, when I was taken aback by Mom staring into my face, and with a sparkle in her eye. She nodded her head toward my fiancée and my two nieces, sitting and laughing together across the yard. Mom took a deep breath in through her nose, like smelling a rose, and said—*said*—with delight, "Doesn't that woman have beautiful children?!"

When we gather as a family now and share stories, that line always gets a laugh. With being so factually wrong, and at the same time so endearingly correct, Mom shared what turned to be the final ray of light to break through her prison of fog. And for a moment, back then, our shady spot on the bench was bathed in a warm glow.

Bill Farmer

Education: B.S., electrical engineering and Japanese, University of Minnesota; M.S., optical and computer-based holography, MIT media lab

Work: Principal consultant at F&A Consulting and adjunct professor at Augsburg University in the Twin Cities. Research engineer at Sharp Corporation in Japan; first foreign member of the technical board of HODIC, a subsidiary of the Japan Society of Physics. Leadership positions at several Twin Cities-based corporations in sales, engineering, and product development. General manager and corporate officer at CyberOptics Corporation. Executive with EAC Product Development Solutions for seven years, leading their consulting practice, until founding F&A in 2016.

Book: *The Power of Habit* by Charles DuHigg

Quote: He that is good at making excuses is seldom good for anything else. —Ben Franklin

More: https://www.linkedin.com/in/billfarmer/

Doing Your Best

Sue Filbin

After my dad returned to Minneapolis from serving in a Marine raider battalion in the Pacific during World War II, his work life was spent with two wholesale electrical companies. He started in the warehouse, moved to the quotations department, and ended his career in sales while also being a sales manager.

When I was in my early teens—an age during which I didn't quite know everything but was old enough to absorb meaningful conversations—I remember my dad telling me, "When you've done your best, you can live with yourself."

I don't recall the circumstances during which this comment was made, nor that my dad elaborated on what he meant, but I've remembered my dad's comment throughout my life and applied my own interpretation to it.

My mom's perspective was similar. After she contracted polio when I was three and my sister was just two months old, from her bed or wheelchair, our mom would instruct us as to how to do dishes, make meals, and perform other household chores. When we needed a hem on a skirt or a treat for an event, we learned to rely on our mom's advice and our own ability to get things done.

I've noticed that in order to do my best, a few things need to be in place. For example, I need to know and respect my personal needs for physical, mental, and financial wellbeing. By taking care of these requirements, I'm better able to contribute to the wellbeing of others. I'm reminded of the warning before an airplane takes off, "…put on your own oxygen mask first before assisting others."

Once I've established a reliable foundation for myself, I've learned how useful it is to understand the expectations of others. By asking questions and listening, I can learn how, or whether, what I have to contribute may be useful.

While I'm grateful for the innate gifts and skills I have, I'm regularly reminded of how much there is to learn and how wrong I can be. This realization leads me to seek out learning opportunities through classes, presentations, conversations, books, online resources, membership in organizations, and other sources.

Another practice I've adopted is to write down what I'm learning as well as what I'm thinking, doing, and aspiring to. These notes aren't profound, and in some cases they're so trite they make me squirm, but they represent the real me. Their actual value is that they enable me to acknowledge any progress I've made, and to reflect on staying with my chosen path with vigor or redirecting my energies.

When I'm engaged in doing my best, I've noticed that I think less about comparing myself to others—which is always a fruitless pursuit—and I've got more gusto to address the lurking presence of my inner critic.

By being prepared to do my best in work-related and personal activities, I've also learned to let go. I recognize that what I have to contribute is not what's required in some circumstances. But when I've done my best, I can live with myself.

Sue Filbin

Education: B.S., design, University of Minnesota

Work: Since 1993, self-employed with my husband at Smiling Dog Design—writing and design for businesses, entrepreneurs, and non-profits. In my earlier youth, I bought printing, sold printing, and ran a printing press; I was a cook and waitress at the Hurry-back Pool and Billiard Hall; and for several years, I had my "dream job" as a mail-carrier in south Minneapolis.

Book: *Life's Greatest Lessons* by Hal Urban

Quote: When you do your best, you can live with yourself. —Bill Summers, my dad

More: smilingdogdesign.com; https://onbeing.org/how-to-listen/

I have never been lost, but I will admit to being confused for several weeks.

DANIEL BOONE

Embrace the Suck!

Doug Fischer

When I think about veterans who have served our nation, I would like to extend my thanks to every veteran for their service to our country. In honor of those who have served, and to keep with my personal theme of **Positivity and Gratitude (aka rhinos are just fat unicorns!)**, I would like to combine the two and talk about a very often-used military expression and mindset, *"Embrace the Suck!"*

What does this mean? Take it from former Army Officer Guy D. McCordle Jr. who answered this question on the website Quora. Essentially, it is a mindset to help our soldiers, sailors, marines, and airmen to keep driving on through tough situations. Some say the expression goes all the way back to William Shakespeare, who wrote, "Let thee embrace me, sour adversity, for wise men say it is the wisest course."

Apparently, life could really suck back in Shakespeare's time as well. The thought process behind embracing the suck is also rooted in Eastern philosophy. Author Anthony Meindl had the following to say about the subject: "It's a very Buddhist concept. When we deny what reality is giving us—what is really happening— then we create suffering. So life is a dance between minimizing expectations and surrendering to what our lives actually reveal to us."

How do you get past repeated physically miserable and

emotionally disturbing situations? Motivational speaker Brendon Burchard tells us how to "embrace the suck." It takes a conscious decision. You must embrace the fact that this misery is your (hopefully temporary) new normal. You accept the fact that this is just the way things are going to be from here on out, and you commit yourself to excellence in this new environment. Simply put, you can't overcome struggle if you hate the struggle. The only way you are going to get through difficult life experiences is by welcoming them (you don't necessarily have to like something to welcome it), and not denying them. So anticipate it, and honor the struggles of achieving your dreams as part of the process.

Don't complain; engage. Don't be surprised; expect the struggles and meet them with your highest self. Engage with the struggles and crappy situations of life as an opportunity to challenge yourself to be present, to be better, to grow.

- To all those who do this—who honor the difficult process of change with optimism—I respect you.
- To those who stand tall and bear life's moments of unfairness and obligation with strength and honor, I encourage you.
- To those who fight hard for your families, doing work or activities that aren't always fun, I support you.
- To the veterans and their families who know struggle more than most, and who give us our freedoms, I honor you.
- To those who feel motivated by a challenge, who care enough to seek excellence, who work through the troubles with a smile, I admire you.

Keep "embracing the suck" day after day, and one day you'll notice that things don't suck so bad anymore!

Doug Fischer

Education: B.S., civil engineering, Iowa State University on a football scholarship

Work: Civil engineer since 1985— Black & Veatch (Kansas City, MO), HNTB (Cleveland, OH), and BRW (Minneapolis). Anoka County engineer since 2002; transportation division manager since 2013.

Book: *Think and Grow Rich* by Napoleon Hill

Quote: Nearly all men can stand adversity, but if you want to test a man's character, give him power. —Abraham Lincoln

More: The Highway Doctor

Optimism is the foundation of courage.
ANONYMOUS

How Can We Empower Our Teens to Become the Hero of Their Own Story?

Ann Marie Forshay

Good News: Optimism and Resilience Can Be Learned.

We are living in an entirely different moment than humankind has ever known. How our teens experience their world and interact has dramatically shifted and we are only beginning to unpack what this involves. The speed of technological advances and the speed of population growth are game changers for humankind and for our planet. The unintended consequences of many of these changes require optimistic, resilient, strong, agile, hopeful, compassionate, and mentally healthy teens and young adults with a strong sense of their own self-efficacy. Yet, one in eight children in the U.S. suffer from an anxiety disorder and the rate is even higher for young adults in college—1:5.

Some teenagers simply are not receiving enough resources from adults to help them to be optimistic and successful. Other teens may have parents who have subscribed to the jet-packed helicopter parenting that leaves kids ill prepared to deal with life.

Take solace. The research is clear and it is good news. Optimism can be learned. Now, more than ever, we need to empower our teens with the tools and role modeling that will position them to be optimistic and become the **heroes of their own stories.**

Let me share with you how my eldest son became the hero of this own story. His story is about how he found a way to change his life from one that felt miserable to one that feels interesting and hopeful.

We were lucky. We found out my son's mood wasn't just down—he was depressed and talking about suicide. It wasn't only anxiety that he was tackling now. When the call came from a trusted family friend, it was an opportunity for the adults in his life to change gears again and wildly up our game.

What we did as adults mattered even more now than ever before. What I, as his mother, needed to figure out was how to navigate through the challenges of the healthcare system, the school system, and the different people in his life so he could find his own way to feel less helpless or hopeless. Ben had endured a lot—the breakup of his family, parents who were dealing with their own challenges after a long marriage, the loss of his home, a new school— and he was being bullied at the same time.

So, what happened? How did Ben become the hero of his own story? It began in middle school, which felt to him both terrible and monotonous. Wake up, go to school, come home and do homework, go to practice, go to bed—lather, rinse, repeat. Ben felt stuck. He began searching for mentors and role models and paying attention to how others approached their own lives—Casey Nystad, Alan Watts, and his grandfather to name a few. Then, Ben decided on a plan to see if his life really was as bad as he felt it was.

So, Ben began an experiment of recording some video everyday. He chose to document things he experienced throughout each day—things he found interesting or funny. On the days in which there was precious little to videotape, he remained determined to still shoot at least some video daily. This determination (what researcher Angela Duckworth calls Grit: The Power of Passion and Perseverance) to document each day led Ben to begin unwittingly to discover small things that he found beautiful or special. He was teaching himself how to savor little moments on less-eventful days. (See Barbara Fredrickson, Positivity: Groundbreaking Research Reveals How to Embrace Positive Emotions.)

Sometimes Ben's video clip from a particular day might be a video of his doing jumps off of a ramp while on his Rollerblades. On other days it might be as simple as wet snow silently falling and clinging to the branches of the trees. At the end of the first year, he edited the video so that he had only a one-second slice of a video clip per day. It was like a scrapbook of the year in video form.

What Ben discovered from compiling the daily video evidence and slicing it down to one second for each day was twofold, and it is an essential part of his own story. He discovered: (1) His life wasn't as monotonous and boring as he thought it was and (2) His life was definitely not as interesting as he wanted it to be.

Ben decided to see more, meet more people, and experience more of what life could offer. So, Ben became an avid mountain biker, a downhill skier, a cliff jumper (breathe, Mama, breathe!), and chose not to be content waiting until high school finished to "start living life." Ben's pursuit became one of growing, learning, and asking questions about how to make life have more depth, more joy, more meaning. His pursuit became about asking questions of himself and his mentors.

Ben continues this project of taking video every day, which he has been doing for six years now. He wanted both to remember these experiences and to reflect on what could be learned from them. When he wrote his essay for his college applications, he chose one word as the title—Balance. It turned out to be crucial to his wishing to strike the right balance between school, friends, job, and mountain biking. When he spent too much time in one area and not enough in the other areas, he did not feel he way he wanted to feel.

Ben is an 18-year old who feels happier now than he can remember feeling. He has become more of a rock climber than a mountain biker this last year. He is in a good place right now and he is proud to be the hero and the architect of his own story. Will he stay in this good place? Life is guaranteed to throw all of us multiple adversities. Some will hit harder than others. There is a sense of peace, though, because Ben has faced difficult challenges and he believes in his ability to figure things out. He collected data that he can be resilient. Ben now shares with others how his one-second video project changed his life. He is truly the **hero of his own story.**

Ann Marie Forshay

Education: B.A., international relations and political science, University of Minnesota; M.A., gerontology, Bethel University; doctoral work in developmental psychology and school psychology, George Mason University

Work: Certified life coach, staff for Senator Dave Durenberger, USAirways, George Mason University, Be the Match, and founder of Forshay Coaching and Consulting.

Book: *How to Have a Good Day: Harness the Power of Behavioral Science to Transform Your Working Life* by Caroline Webb

Quote: My mission in life is not merely to survive, but to thrive; and to do so with some passion, some compassion, some humor, and some style. —Maya Angelou

More: www.forshaycoaching.com

The world is full of magic things,
patiently waiting for our senses to grow sharper.
W. B. YEATS

An Outlook of Optimism.
It's Just Around the Corner.
Bob Freytag

It's impossible to know what's next, and it's nearly impossible to keep going if you don't have an optimistic view of the world when things get tough. I mean really tough. Sometimes you need to know (or at least believe) there's something better just around the corner. As an entrepreneur, there have been plenty of times when I had no idea where the next dollar was coming from or if I was going to be able to make payroll next month.

When life and business are rolling right along on an upswing, optimism and happiness are all around. When the cycle goes the other way—and it always does—your attitude and beliefs are what drive you, and that's when optimism is critical. That's when "something better is just ahead" must be kept in mind. Be careful not to view the world only through rose-colored glasses; don't fool yourself into believing something that isn't there. You have got to keep it in perspective. You'll have plenty of opportunities to question yourself and those around you. You'll lie awake at night wondering where the next customer, employee, opportunity is coming from. That's when optimism and perseverance are your friend and will keep driving you forward.

Bob Freytag

Education: B.A., art & design, Iowa State University

Work: President of Introworks 1992-present. Leadership, executive and volunteer roles for a number of profit and nonprofit organizations including St. Jude Children's Research Hospital, The Rotary Club of Minneapolis, Professional Referral Organization, Sales and Marketing Executives of Minneapolis/St. Paul, and The CEO Roundtable.

Book: *Start With Why* by Simon Sinek

Quote: We judge others by their actions. We judge ourselves by our intentions. —Anonymous

More: www.intro.works

https://www.linkedin.com/in/bobfreytag/

Creativity is intelligence having fun.
ALBERT EINSTEIN

The School Dropout

Allen L. Gerdin

Daydreaming was a favorite pastime throughout many of my years. Most of it was done during school time, which had an effect on what should have been accomplished. It was only in the first few years of school that there was some pride in bringing a report card home. Poor study habits and a lack of reading skills magnified the situation during the freshman year in high school. Early in the sophomore year, when freshman English had to re-taken, it appeared best to discontinue any further schooling. This decision was finalized when the English teacher harshly criticized my abilities in front of all my classmates and instructed me go to the office of the superintendent.

Two years later, the English teacher married the science teacher, who also coached all sports. She then was not allowed to teach. This gave me the motivation to return to school, only if the requirement to re-take freshman English was dropped. My feelings were very optimistic that I would be able to then complete the three remaining years of schooling, and be able to graduate. On graduation day, the-then teacher of senior English informed me that she should have given me a failing grade but did not want to endure another year with me in her class. I thanked her for that and told her that now having a high school diploma, I would never set my foot in another school.

The next two years were spent helping on the home farm and doing day labor for many of the neighboring farmers. Then a severe knee injury while doing custom work for one of the farmers made it almost impossible to remain in that line of work. At that time, a local manufacturing company of farm machinery was looking for help during a short period of the season. This transitioned into full-time employment for me for the next five years that ended with being asked to purchase the department of the company that was under my management. However, prior to this, my wife and I had been discussing some other possibilities. I had told her that I always wished that I was smart enough to go to college and get a "good" job. She told me, without hesitation, "You *are* smart enough, if you apply yourself." That was the needed motivation to begin the college application process. We chose the University of Minnesota, which accepted me with probationary provisions.

For some reason—maybe optimism and applying myself—college was much easier than high school. I made the dean's honor roll during the first year in college, and even one quarter with a 23-credit-load plus working 20-25 hours per week at the same time. A teaching assistant position was offered to me in my senior year for one of my required classes, a class in farm machinery. It was a very special privilege to help teach a class I had to take for course credit, and also get paid for doing it. Eventually, this background led to a teaching position at the University of Minnesota School of Agriculture in Crookston, MN.

If it is conceivable, and believable, it is achievable.

Optimism is the catalyst.

Al Gerdin

Education: B.S., agricultural education

Work: Mostly in sales of turf equipment and related supplies.

Book: *Choosing Civility* by Dr. P. M. Forni

Quote: Natural talents are gifts for three reasons. First, you don't have to earn them—they came with your birth. Second, they are gifts because you get something for yourself when you give them away. Third, they are a gift to others because they get something from you that is theirs to keep. —Richard Leider

Quote: The meaning of life is to find your gift. The purpose of life is to give it away! —Pablo Picasso

The best way out of a difficulty is through it.
ANONYMOUS

Mentorship

Gary Havir

We were encouraged, prodded, cajoled, kiddingly threatened, mildly harassed and a whole lot more by our Roseville Area Optimist Club. They wanted our thoughts to create a book from our membership—from the heart. The purpose of this is to share some thoughts that might have some value to others.

I have to admit, this was not an easy project for me to start. Then it dawned on me, the essence of my procrastination. Simply, there are so many individuals whom I admire. These individuals are more worthy than I to give you great thoughts. Each of them has been instrumental in my journey of life. Others have taught me, inspired me and are responsible for my now-what-I'll-call a phenomenal life. Not without many bumps and bruises, but I am fortunate because of others who have surrounded me.

Hence you have now figured out "mentorship" is paramount for anyone and everyone. Learn from others, at all times. In addition, help mentor others along the way. Both things are important to success.

Several of my mentors will be mentioned. Unfortunately, there are way too many. For those who are not listed, my guess is they will not be hurt. It's been my experience that mentors are oblivious to the fact they are even mentors.

There are so many role models in my life. I was fortunate to have a great family and realize this is not the case for all. Obviously, this gave me a great foundation to build upon. The basics were in place. However, my father got really sick when I was in the sixth grade, and he was no longer able to work. Thankfully, he lived for quite a few more years, but not without many trips to Mayo Clinic.

We were not destitute by any means. We no longer were able to do what we did prior to his illness. The finances were pretty much drained. My mother became the glue, went to work and held things together. I fibbed about my age and started working to make ends meet.

Forgive me as I have to share a side note about my mother. When she was 92, she was robbed at gunpoint in her home. I went to her house to console her—or maybe myself—as I was angry that someone could do such a thing. Bless her soul. Her comment to me was, "I feel bad for the guy who robbed me. He probably had small kids and a family to support and really needed the money." See what I mean about a good upbringing?

Here is where the mentoring starts, and why I am a big proponent of schools. Mr. Amdahl, my sixth-grade teacher, was my very early mentor. He realized things were not quite the same at home. Somehow, I latched onto his every word. Interestingly, one of our projects was investing in the stock market. My pick was a company called Control Data, whose stock price soared. After my schooling, I went to work for Control Data. Eventually I moved on to a career in insurance and financial services which I think was a result of my sixth-grade class on finance. Thank you, Mr. Amdahl!

Next it was on to high school. There were two teachers who really inspired me. Again, I was still a bit bitter because of my father's situation. Mr. Burns was my band teacher. He was the one who allowed me to appreciate music. This was one of my escapes from the everyday challenges. Because of him, we started a rock band called Yesterdays Children, which was going to be my ultimate career. Once I realized rock was not going to pay the bills, I recognized music will always be a great release.

Then Mr. Olson came along. He had a brand new program called "distributive education." This class allowed me to continue my schooling and be able to work. More importantly, Mr. Olson's class taught me the art of sales and relationships which is a staple for all of society.

On to my working world. There are many who have inspired me. At the top of the list has to be Mr. Fred Jarosz. He was the chief marketing officer for Horace Mann. Horace Mann is the insurance and financial services company I have now represented for almost 40 years. His tagline was "Pursuit of Excellence." He mentored me by being tough, and always assuming there was more that could be done to achieve this Pursuit of Excellence. No matter how tough the conversation, at the end he would always kind of give you a light thump on the chest and say, "Just remember, there is no one better than you, and because of this you can accomplish anything." If you knew Fred, you would feel exactly the same, as he taught people to believe anyone can move mountains.

Recently, my newest mentor is Don Salverda. He is the founder of the Roseville Area Optimist Club. You probably guessed, he was the one after me to complete this project. He has created energy within the Optimist Club due to his passion. Recently, he also started the Optimist Book Club. This book club means a great deal to me and the books are a big help with life. Each member of the club has inspired me, and I consider them all mentors, too.

Not mentioning my wife Win and son Max as mentors would be negligent of me. Both of them are always there to help me every day. They are the reason for me to want to improve daily.

Well, who would have thought I could actually get this done? Somehow, my mentors were instrumental with this, too. Go figure!

Gary Havir

Education: Computer technology, Control Data Institute

Work: President and agency owner of Educators Insurance Resource Services, Inc., for almost 40 years—a financial services and insurance firm that represents Horace Mann, which specializes in working with educators.

Book: *Daily Stoic* by Ryan Holiday and Stephen Hanselman

Quote: Do the right things. —Anonymous

On Being an Optimist in the World Today

Jon Heyer

How many of you pay attention to the media? We all do to some extent. We have social media, print media, and broadcast media—radio and TV. The media just loves to put things out there for us, and if you pay attention, most of what they put out is negative. The message that they give us is the sky is falling, everything is dire, the world is going to end, and we are all going to die. That is the message the media pounds into us, day after day after day.

The reaction of people to this constant media bombardment is to be like Eeyore from the *Winnie the Pooh* stories, to say, "Oh bother, woe is me." Many of us start embracing that negativity and those depressing messages. I am an optimist, and in the face of all this media negative pressure, it is hard to be an optimist. But what you need to do is to trust your experience, to open your eyes and ears, and notice what is really going on around you.

You can overcome media negativity if you can just inform yourself. I am going to illustrate lots of cases that support the case for optimism. I remember crawling under the desk, head down, during fallout drills in grade school. We thought the Russians were going to nuke us. Guess what? That didn't happen. We were told there was a new ice age coming in the '70s, but that never happened either. We were told there were diseases that would decimate the world's population—polio, smallpox, strains of influenza, Ebola, and even AIDs. The world's population is now higher than it ever has been. The diseases didn't kill us off. We were told that temperatures would rise dramatically, the ice caps would melt, and all of the cities on the coasts would be flooded. This was all supposed to have happened already. There is still ice at the poles—as much as ever. At last check, New York and Miami are still high and dry.

The media tries to scare us, but if we allow our observations to take over and inform us, we can fight back that negative media influence and be optimistic for the future. Look at the habits of people today. We have light bulbs that burn 10% of the electricity that we used 20 years ago. We drive cars that are almost emission free and now we are moving toward electric and hybrid cars that will further reduce emissions. A number of years ago, our state instituted an emissions-testing program and it was eliminated because none of the new cars ever failed; they simply did not emit a significant amount of pollutants. We have cleaner water and cleaner air—thanks in part to good legislation— than we did 50 years ago. There are more trees in America now than there were 200 years ago. These are facts, but you have to look to see them.

Yes, there are parts of the world that are being deforested and there are parts of the world that have pollution problems, but we can control only what we can control. What is seen is that in our part of the world, we are doing better than we were before. When you drive down our streets, every week people have blue recycling bins at the curb. We did not do that 20 years ago. Everything we threw away went to landfills. We are reducing the amount of garbage placed in our landfills by half. Yet we still have the media hammering us with the message that we are going to die and the world is going to end, all because we are treating the earth so terribly.

Franklin Delano Roosevelt once said, "We have nothing to fear but fear itself." We are being made afraid by what we hear. I challenge you to watch the news for a week and take notice of the negativity. Every day they lead off with murder and pollution and dire events. They even try to scare us with the weather. We might have a snowstorm, as little as two inches. Look, it is Minnesota, what do you expect? We all need to open our eyes, open our ears, and notice our experiences. Inform yourself and you can be optimistic about our future. You can make this world the best place that you can. You can be positive and optimistic. When you get out of bed in the morning, you have a choice between two of the *Winnie the Pooh* characters. You can be Eeyore, and embrace negativity, saying, "Oh bother, woe is me" or can you can be Tigger and bounce with joy and do your best in the world today. The choice is yours.

Jon Heyer

Education: B.A., psychology, University of Minnesota; M.A., theology, Saint Catherine University

Work: Semi-retired religious educator, 35+ years experience. Currently working part-time at St. Odilia Church. Part-time professional musician.

Book recommendation: *The River of Doubt* by Candice Millard

More: Heyer4house.com Elephantintheroomband.com

Follow Your Dreams, Live a Balanced Life and Look at the Sunny Side

Joel Huser

My early life growing up was on a dairy farm. I attended a one-room country school for the first two years of grade school. After that I attended a small public school in Lester Prairie with a total enrollment of 250 from grades 1 to 12. I participated in sports but my primary interest was music. I played trombone and participated in many solo contests and regional band events. After high school, I attended the University of Minnesota and played in the football marching band for two years.

My plan for college was to study the biological sciences. However, the academic training I received at my small high school was not advanced enough to prepare me for the challenges of the science programs at the University of Minnesota. My plans had to change to a less-challenging curriculum. Unfortunately, I also became more socially active which distracted from my education. I often drifted from the lifestyle more well suited to me to one that I saw others doing. I regret the lack of discipline and focus on my education during the time of studying for my college degree at the U of M.

After graduating, I worked for two years and decided I was not satisfied with the work I was doing. Fortunately, I was able to return to college with more focus and discipline and graduate with an M.B.A. in accounting. I was able to enjoy a career in finance and accounting for 40 years.

My family life included three children. We enjoyed life together doing many outdoor activities including time at the lake. Unfortunately, one of my children died at an early age. I also lost my wife to cancer after 43 years of marriage. I was very fortunate to meet a woman who had similar circumstances and interests as I did and I am now enjoying a second marriage. My experience has reinforced the value of enjoying life every day and spending every possible moment with family and friends.

I have a strong belief in the value of the religious community in living a good life. I think a belief in a supreme being (in Christian religion it is Jesus Christ) is important to a having a healthy body and soul. Being a part of a Christian community is both spiritually uplifting and socially healthy.

In summary, I believe it is very important to have balance in work, family and community. Always follow your dreams and live the life that is best for you. Avoid distractions from others that may keep you from achieving your dreams. Always be ready to learn so you can stay current with the change that is constant in our world. And always look at the sunny side!

Joel Huser

Education: B.S., agriculture economics, University of Minnesota; M.B.A., accounting, St. Cloud State University

Work: University of Minnesota Extension Service; finance and accounting career working at several companies in various positions.

Book: *All We Have Is All We Need* by Karen Casey

We are all of us richer than we think we are.
MICHEL DE MONTAIGNE

Optimism is a Marathon

Craig Johnson

A glass half full, always seeing the upside, not letting things get you down may be generally considered the attitude of what it means to be an optimist to those who are not. In my opinion, optimists have our bad days as well, but we see the potential of what is to come. Sure, it would be great if we never had bad days, however, if that were truly the case, then I am not sure which would be truer—that we are delusional or that we are as delusional as others would make us out to be.

There are going to be bad events, bad days, bad weeks even, but things get better. This realization is what makes me an optimist. During the bad times, people take the time to mourn and self-assess, and this is normal. However, optimists at the end of the assessment period realize it is time to plan a course of action that improves the situation.

This plan of action starts with the idea that things will get better and that we can make a difference not only in our own life, but also for those around us. Be it family, friends, co-workers, or acquaintances, for things to become better, actions must be taken. This typically doesn't happen with a glorious unshakeable plan, but rather a solid workable plan that can be taken one step at a time. And as things start to get better, the next steps are taken, and before you know it, you wonder what all the fuss was about.

Optimism is not a sprint; it is not something that magically appears by attending a conference or reading a book, but it is a way of looking at life and the pursuit of a higher level of being. As with most things that become great and sustainable, being an optimist is a marathon. If you keep plugging along, push through the walls and keep moving, the goal gets closer and a better life is actualized for the optimist and those who surround them.

Craig Johnson

Education: B.S., civil engineering, University of Minnesota Institute of TechnologyWork

Work: Rani Engineering, Inc., director of operations since 2014.

Book: *Good to Great* by Jim Collins

Quote: Unless someone like you cares a whole awful lot, nothing is going to get better. It's not. —The Lorax (Dr. Seuss)

More: www.linkedin.com/in/craig-johnson-RaniEng-DirOfOps

My Days as a Farmer:
Set Goals and Track for Success

Peggy Johnson

The summer before ninth grade, I became a farmer. A cucumber farmer. A pickle farmer to be exact. My family had just moved to a new home in the country set on five acres. We were about 10 miles from the town where I previously lived and six miles from the new town where I started school just after Christmas break. This new town had a Gedney pickle factory that employed kids looking for summer work. Since we had acreage, my dad decided his daughters would have their own crop. Dad designated one acre of our land for pickle farming. The Gedney pickle factory provided the seeds while we provided the labor. All summer, cucumbers were harvested, delivered to town, and sold at fair-market value.

I was a hard worker, yet I had no idea of the potential income available from my labors, so every day was torture. I do believe if I had had a goal and tracked it, the process would have been more rewarding. As it was, I saw only effort and sacrifice. If I understood the potential from my efforts, I would have had a better attitude. If I had seen the big picture from the start, I'm sure my enthusiasm would have been different.

Every day that summer, I worked hard as a farmer. And every day I resented the hard work—cultivating, planting, weeding, and eventually harvesting. I blindly went through the entire process without a plan and without any financial goals. I worked hard (mostly because my parents made me), and I was frustrated and angry about all the hard work.

At the end of the summer we had, indeed, made some serious cash. So much, in fact, that I forgot about my anger and signed up to be a pickle farmer again the next year. But I learned something that first year as a frustrated farmer: I learned the importance of having a plan—to set a goal and have a purpose, an objective. With a monetary goal for that next summer and a time commitment outlined, I was able to focus on my farming tasks and celebrate the progress without anger and frustration. Clarity of my goals provided me with choices and options, and I felt empowered. I had discovered greater peace and enjoyed being a farmer, so much so that I did it for three more seasons.

Peggy Johnson

Education: AAS degree, surveying and civil technology, St. Paul Technical Vocational Institute (now St. Paul College)

Work: Owner of Pointmap Incorporated for 25 years.

Book: *Made to Stick: Why Some Ideas Survive and Others Die* by Chip Heath and Dan Heath

Quote: *If opportunity doesn't knock, build a door* —Milton Berle

More: pointmap@pointmap.com
https://www.linkedin.com/in/pegjohnson/

Do Your Best Every Day—
Advice to My Children
Michelle Julius

As the mother of two teenage children, I am often trying to think of the best advice I can share with them to avoid the mistakes I made—and live the best life they can live. I just want them to be happy! But as I am also learning, and remembering back to when I was a teenager, we all have to make our own mistakes and discover our own path! So as much as we talk as a family, I try not to get discouraged when they prefer not to take my advice and do their own thing. Because I want them to be the best individual they can be—on their own terms—to be happy and proud of their life.

As a teenager and young adult, I definitely did not make the best choices. I was determined to go to college—but had to work very hard to get average grades. It took me five years, but I earned a civil engineering degree. I was so ready to get to work in construction. The economy was not great when I graduated college, so a move to Chicago for a job offer was an unexpected turn. But I am so grateful now for the tremendous experience. I learned a lot about myself as a person, as well as the type of company and individuals that I want to work with—and for—during my career.

When we decided to move to Minnesota in June 1999, it was a huge leap. My husband had a job offer, but I was eight-months pregnant with our first child. So we took a leap and moved, hopeful that I would find something after our son was born. It was a very strange three months for me. I had never been without a job before! But for me, I was moving home, and was happy to be close to family and friends.

In September 1999, I started as a temporary employee with a local firm on a six-month contract as a construction engineer. The company hired me as a full-time employee after my contract, and I have been there ever since. I have remained with the same company for over 18 years—through three mergers and acquisitions. I am now part of a publicly traded, global company with over 90,000 employees. I worked very hard and moved my way up in the organization, managing more staff and projects. I would volunteer to help out on initiatives and anything I could get my hands on. As those above me left the company for other opportunities, I would volunteer to take over their tasks, and in many cases was promoted into their positions. I was willing to learn anything—and wanted to learn as much as I could. The more experience I had, the more I felt I could help the company succeed.

I was promoted to vice president at 36 years old. I remain one of the younger VPs and one of a few women in my position. I continue to deal with both age and gender challenges in my daily work life—especially with people who have not worked with me before—in a very male-dominated industry that seems to think you need 40-plus years of experience for anyone to listen.

I have always prided myself on hard work. I was not able to put in the long hours in the office that some engineers did, with small kids at home and a husband who has a very demanding career that requires lots of travel as well. So I learned early to work very efficiently and effectively! I worked in the office, and at home—wherever I could—to get the work done. I pride myself on being responsive to my client's needs, as well as to my co-workers. I return calls and emails quickly. I am extremely diligent about working my calendar. Meetings, travel time, family time, and learning time—all are on my calendar! I am protective of my personal time and make it a priority. I have always said that people make time for what they want to make time for…so the "I'm-too-busy" excuse is an expression that I do not take well from people.

I always meet deadlines, and pride myself on quality work. And I take pride in attending all my children's events! As I sent my oldest off to college this year, I realized how quickly time passes and I am so glad that I protected my family time to attend their events!

As a family, we are active in our church, participating in several mission trips, and a variety of other volunteer positions. We are active with our childrens' sports-team booster clubs. And we strive to live healthy lives and exercise daily. And sleep is a must!

Never stop learning, never stop growing, and always be yourself! Treat others as you want to be treated. Be proud of your life, your family, and your work.

Michelle Julius

Education: B.S., civil engineering, University of Wisconsin—Platteville

Professional: Vice president, AECOM, Minneapolis, MN, 1999-present; construction engineer, Benchmark Construction, Chicago, IL.

Book: *When Generations Collide and The M Factor*, both by Lynne C. Lancaster and David Stillman

Quote: Be the change you want to see in the world. —Mahatma Gandhi

I have great faith in a seed. Convince me that you have a seed there, and I am prepared to expect wonders.

HENRY DAVID THOREAU

Be Willing to Sacrifice
to Follow a New Dream

Nora Keenan

After teaching high school students biology for 16 years, I felt the call of a new dream—working in a career that involved health research. While I loved biology as a subject area and enjoyed working with high school students and loved the spirit of a high school community, I was also weary of teaching the same material four or five times a day year after year. Helping students focus microscopes or dissect preserved animals became a burden even though it had previously been a fun part of teaching biology.

Some years I would be able to teach an advanced biology class and that allowed some change in the content material and I did relish that opportunity. I did try to make it work. I earned a master's degree in secondary education with a concentration in science education and continued to take summer courses in areas like outdoor education to keep my courses as interesting as possible for the students ... and for me.

At first, I did not receive encouragement to follow my dream. Others discouraged me from changing careers by saying that I was good at teaching and warning me that the grass is always greener somewhere else. Over time, my family was really supportive and very proud that I had the courage and perseverance to make a mid-life career change to do something I loved.

After a few years of thinking about leaving teaching, I enrolled in a course that dealt with making a career change. One of the main tenets of the course was that a person did not have to go back to school to change careers. We were supposed to be able to identify a new career that used our skill set and fulfilled our career goals. By the end of the course, the instructors told me that that concept did not apply to me because a career in health research would require additional education.

Reaching my dream career took seven years and involved earning two advanced degrees, moving to two different states, and incurring significant student loans. It required many types of sacrifices, but the end result was well worth it: a position as an epidemiologist at the Centers for Disease Control and Prevention (CDC), a federal agency located in Atlanta, Georgia. It was thrilling for me to start a new career at age 48 and to be working with others to improve the health of our nation. Most of my 19 years at CDC were in the Division of Heart Disease and Stroke Prevention within the National Center for Chronic Disease Control and Prevention.

It was also very satisfying to go back to school as an older-than-average student, and to enter a whole new realm of knowledge and practice as well as meeting other students from all over the world. The experiences that went along with earning degrees at two different institutions in two different states broadened my perspectives in ways that I could not have imagined when I anticipated following my dream.

Nora Keenan

Education: B.S., biology major, chemistry minor, secondary education minor; M.A., secondary education with concentration in science education; M.P.H., epidemiology; Ph.D., epidemiology

Work: High school biology teacher at St. Agnes High School in St. Paul, Totino-Grace High School in Fridley, Columbus High School in Waterloo, Iowa, and Archbishop Brady High School in St. Paul; epidemiologist at the National Center for Chronic Disease Prevention and Control at the Centers for Disease Control and Prevention (CDC) in Atlanta, Georgia for 19 years.

Recommended book: *Grant* by Ron Chernow

Quote: Do unto others as you would have them do unto you. —Matthew 7:12

If your actions inspire others to dream more, do more and become more, you are a leader.
JOHN QUINCY ADAMS

Has Anyone Ever Told You *No*?!

Dick Klick

I hope someone has told you **no**…so you could figure out your next step. That is if you *really* wanted to complete the project—or even start it. I have heard **no** from U of MN academia many times. I heard **no** from an OEM manufacturer (original equipment manufacturer) that I represented for over 30 years. I was told **yes** by a customer who bought several thousand trucks from me.

When I first started at the U of M, my high school academics prep was liberal arts. The classes I wanted to take at the U of M were in engineering. Every U of M advisor told me **no,** that I wasn't qualified to take the classes I wanted. Now what could I do to take the classes I wanted?

- First, I studied the U of M catalogue for exceptions.
- Then I asked advice from the dean of the college in which I wanted to take classes.
- I promised the dean I would study hard if I could take the class for which I was registering.
- The dean signed off on my class-exception enrollment. The dean did this for me for all my classes in industrial engineering. I had to meet with him and explain why I wanted the class every quarter and every semester.
- In one of my meetings with the dean, he explained that I had a problem. He stated that the University was there to grant degrees and that I was only there to learn!

How many classes did I take? All of the industrial engineering classes offered in the 1960s and '70s. I even taught a laboratory class in designing a machine shop set-up. I used the Minneapolis Society for the Blind for a reference (I worked there part time).

What did this time at the U of M teach me? I learned how to negotiate and how to meet objectives.

In the late '70s, I worked as a fleet sales manager for an OEM of trucks. A customer wanted me to make modifications to trucks for their specific use. The OEM didn't want to make a special truck for them. I was told **no** by operations, **no** by manufacturing, and **no** by sales management. I was constantly told it was too risky, unproven, and had an unknown fiscal benefit. (I was even fired twice!)

So…I went to work.

- I found marketing and operations department heads at the OEM who would help and encourage me.
- I found a similar outdated modification on another chassis built by this OEM with many failures.
- I contracted with a small shop to build a prototype.
- We brought the project in-house. We modified and improved the other prototypes.
- It took only five years for the first prototype and two years for the second chassis prototype.
- I sent a chassis to the Vehicle Test Facility in Mesa, AZ, for New Vehicle Modification Certification to comply with Federal Highway Safety Standards. We discovered what the OEM did wrong and were able to correct the braking system!
- The customer wanted us to supply them with 60 to 70 of our modified chassis per year. We didn't have the manpower or facility.

Finally, the OEM admitted that production was possible. I helped the OEM set up on their site a mod-shop to build these modified chassis for us and for additional customers. To date, several thousand have been built and used safely on our highways since 1989.

After 30 years, I retired from the OEM. I became bored with retirement and started an independent life and health insurance agency—after people told me **no** I shouldn't. I was too old! I went back to the U of M in the 2000s for the third time. I finally received my B.S. I needed my B.S. for certain insurance products. No negotiations were allowed! I have been continuing to expand my agency for the past six years and currently represent nine insurance companies.

Dick Klick

Education: Associate degree; B.S., multidiscipline (mathematics, communications, and history), University of Minnesota

Work History: U.S. Navy, electronic tech, flight crew; electronic tech, Honeywell; sub-contract procurement, Minneapolis Society for the Blind (Vision Loss Resources); Travelers Life Insurance Agent; National Car Rental truck division; started Fontaine Truck Equipment, Roseville Diesel, and Mack Trucks & Twin City Mack Trucks, fleet manager, VP sales, and minority owner; since 2010, Richard Frank Klick Agency, independent life, health, and retirement agency.

Book: *Man's Search for Meaning* by Viktor E. Frankl

Quote: As one's thinking is, such as one becomes.
—From Sanskrit

More: www.rfkinvest.com

Everything can be taken from a man but one thing:
the last of the human freedoms—to choose one's attitude
in any given set of circumstances; to choose one's own way.

VIKTOR E. FRANKL

Life is Easy When You're on Top of the Mountain

Jim Knuckey

"Life is easy when you're up on the mountain
And you've got peace of mind like you've never known.
But when things change and you're down in the valley,
Don't lose faith, for you're never alone.

For the God on the mountain is still God in the valley.
When thing go wrong, He'll make it right.
And the God of the good times
is still the God of the bad times.
The God of the day is still God in the night.

We talk of faith when we're up on the mountain.
Oh, but the talk comes easy, when life's at its best.
But it's down in the valley of trials and temptation
That's when faith is really put to the test.

God of the Mountain is my favorite hymn. Life is a never-ending series of ups and downs. Staying optimistic is critical for overcoming the bumps. There is absolutely nothing positive to gain from being negative. You cannot allow your mind to head in that direction. Your positive attitude will not only help you but will also help others with whom you come in contact.

In the twilight of my life, I'm thinking back to some of the things that have impacted and reinforced my positive attitude with life.

The first important event came at age seventeen. I had spent the summer working in a girl's summer camp as kitchen boy. In my time off I would work hard getting in shape for football in the fall. I would run five miles after work and do another forty-five minutes of exercises. My health and physical condition were more than excellent.

I was excited when camp was over. I was high on the mountain. The next thing I knew I was in a hospital not knowing what had happened to me. Neither did the doctors. That first day in the hospital, I slowly felt my body stiffen up. By the next morning I was completely paralyzed except I could see and talk. Ten days later, doctors told me that I had Guillain-Barré syndrome, a disease that affects muscles. I was very lucky. This disease usually has lasting paralysis for most people. I was fortunate to be able to look at a crucifix on the wall at the end of my bed. A retired nun came in daily and prayed with me. If it wasn't for that spiritual support, I don't know if I would have ever fully recovered. My brain was stuffed full of negative thoughts: Would I ever play football and hockey again? Would I ever walk? Would I be in a wheelchair? Could I work?—on and on with negative thoughts.

A week or so later, the disease left my body completely and I was released from the hospital, fully recovered. That afternoon I showed up at school and told the coach "I'm here." He told me go suit up and get on the practice field. That coming Friday night, I played my first game, 35 pounds lighter than the day I entered the hospital. I was still up on the mountain.

I truly believe that the crucifix of the Lord and the little old nun showed me that He was there for me. That faith has been life-long.

Sports have had more than a share of my life's ups and downs. After I was able to get back on the football field, I soon found out we had lost four games in a row and we were headed for a complete losing season. As part of this experience, four of our key players got hurt and were sidelined for the rest of the season. Three close friends quit the team because they couldn't handle losing. I definitely was down from high to low in the valley. I went home and told my mother that I wanted to quit the team. I don't remember ever seeing her so angry. She told me there were no quitters in the family and I would not be the first. She emphasized all this by telling me, "To get my rear out to the practice field and quit whining, and don't let the door hit you in the rear end." I quickly learned that quitting in life was not an option very often, and it should not be for me.

Football game five was with Superior Central, 1953 Wisconsin State Champions. Before the game, I could tell my teammates were not exactly happy about this opportunity. I, too, was still in the funk. As usual we had a prayer session before the game. I asked the Lord to give me the strength to perform to the best of my ability. He was with me, after being down two touchdowns near half time.

I was playing nose tackle on defense. I noticed Superior's center moving the ball on the ground. In those days, that was against the rules. When I saw the ball move, I put my shoulder into the center and recovered his fumble. I did this again a little while later. When I came off the field the second time, the team mobbed me. As I reflected later, our team to the man had something to be excited about—that we could do something to be proud of. Our team developed a different outlook for the rest of the season on football life. For me, I was high on the mountain again. By the end of the season, we all had a better view of ourselves. I certainly did.

When you're down in the valley, don't sell yourself short. You have more inner drive than you think. Stay optimistic.

Three more short stories:

Our three-year-old granddaughter had a non-malignant brain tumor removed. As a result, a portion of her brain was removed. Our family didn't even know if she would live. Her full recovery took years. At age 20, she was almost fully recovered. At age 23 she has two college degrees—one from a junior college with a straight-A average. This year she graduated from Northern Iowa University where she made the Dean's List. From being in the valley, she has more than proved herself and has climbed the mountain.

Another granddaughter didn't think she was smart enough to go to college to obtain a four-year degree, so she went to a vocational school. She earned three two-year degrees in hospital administration. She was on the Dean's List every semester with nearly a straight-A average. Now she knows she is smart and can go back to school to receive her four-year degree in two years.

Number-one grandson is a very healthy young man. At age 24, he suffered a tragic back stroke four years ago. He is paralyzed from the waist to the bottom of feet. Through aggressive rehabilitation through The ABLE Program at Allina Courage Kenny Institute in Golden Valley, MN, he has made great strides in recovery. He was awarded a $5,000 scholarship to establish a business. He now has a thriving business as a fishing guide and builder of custom fishing rods. Will he ever recover so he can walk again? Only time will tell. Medicine is moving at a very fast past. The solution to walk and reduce pain in his legs may be just around the corner. He is a driven, focused person. He will make it up the mountain.

I share these stories with you so you will never, never lose hope. Stay positive. You never know when He will answer your prayers.

Thank you for allowing me to share my stories.

Jim Knuckey

Education: Architectural design, Salter Vocational School, Duluth, Minnesota; business, University of Minnesota, Duluth; commercial electrical and lighting design, Dunwoody Institute, Minneapolis, Minnesota

Work: Lighting and electrical designer for a mechanical, electrical consulting firm; sales coaching, mentoring, and marketing in lighting sales and energy management; for 22 years, owned and operated with my wife and another couple one of the largest publishers and distributors of wildlife art in the country; past president of Minnesota Jaycees; former national VP of the US Jaycees.

Book: *Essentialism* by Greg McKeown

Quote: Walk softly and carry a big stick. —Teddy Roosevelt

You Can Catch More Flies With Honey Than With Vinegar

Stephen Manweiler

My mother always advised me to approach others in a polite, respectful manner in the same way I would like to be treated because it makes going through life easier and more positive. People respond more cooperatively and are more likely to be helpful if you treat them well.

One would think this should be standard practice due to good old common sense, but I have found that many people do not follow this advice. The current political climate in the United States seems to glorify crass, rude and downright mean behavior. The moniker "Ugly American" fits so many people these days that it's almost scary, certainly disheartening. At times I feel ashamed to be a citizen of a country that revels in being crude. I certainly do not want to be around these people. Far from projecting strength, rude behavior reflects barbarism, defensiveness, weakness and total lack of sophistication.

When I worked for a biotech company years ago, people would call to complain about our products. Sometimes the caller would explain logically what was wrong, which made understanding their situation easier. Not infrequently they had been sold the wrong version of the product to control their target pest. This meant I could contact the seller and recommend a refund or exchange depending upon the desires of the caller. Sellers usually honored my requests. A few callers were nasty on the phone. Other than knowing they were angry, I could not understand their problem and circumstances which usually resulted in me not recommending any remedial action. Those callers lost out because they could not communicate an intelligible description of their problem.

Three years ago, a colleague and I were stuck in Lansing, Michigan. Our flight home had been canceled due to bad weather. The afternoon of the next day we were in line at the airport ticket counter as the last departure to Detroit was boarding. The man in front of us was bawling out the ticket agent while she was trying to scan boarding passes for passengers boarding the flight. I asked him to let her process the passengers because it would take only minutes and certainly would not delay those of us in line much longer. He snarled and quieted down until the door to the Detroit-bound flight closed. The ticket agent then told the man that she had two seats left on a Minneapolis-bound itinerary the next day. He barked that he did not want any "bleeping" seat on their airline, so she gave him a refund that he took and walked away. My colleague and I also needed to return to Minneapolis. When she turned to us, I asked if we could have those two seats. We had them in five minutes, along with a discount coupon for a decent hotel next to the airport. I hope I helped make her day a little better. She certainly helped my colleague and me. It was win-win for sure.

I try to put myself in the shoes of the person with whom I am interacting. I want a good outcome for myself and for them, too. I try to let them know I don't blame them for my problem—I simply want their help solving my problem. Try it. It frequently works, and it certainly makes life easier and much more positive.

Stephen Manweiler

Education: Ph. D., entomology (biological control), University of California-Berkeley; leadership and effective management training, Hamline University Center for Public Administration; leadership training, Don Salverda and Associates

Work: Metropolitan Mosquito Control District executive director April 2014 to present. Director, operations and technical services, eight years; technical services coordinator, nine years. Previously, biosys*, a biological pest-control company, manager of inventory and production planning; manager, International Nematode Products; senior entomologist, urban pest control program, department statistician.

Book: *Choosing Civility: The Twenty-five Rules of Considerate Conduct* by P. F. Forni

Quote: Don't forget to smell the roses (enjoy something every day). — My mother

* The spelling of this company's name with a lower-case "b" is correct.

The Design Inside

David McKnight

It was Christmas Eve and our family was taking turns opening presents, as is the tradition in our house. My daughter handed me a present saying, "Open this one, Dad." She had purchased the gift, and by the smile on her face, she was excited about her selection. It was a book entitled *The Story*. While I like the book, what was most precious was the inscription she had written inside the cover, "Thank you for helping me understand how my story fits within His story."

My daughter is twenty-one, but the story began many years earlier, when she was about three years old. At the time my work as a consultant was helping me understand that there is a "design" in each of us. This design reflects the way we see the world, how we take in information, and how we process it—in short, how we behave. I witnessed the evidence of this in hundreds of people with whom I have worked. I had begun to believe that there is a script or design already written in each one of us, which is evident from an early age. We often just need someone to help us read our script.

As my daughter grew from babyhood to a young child, I began to try to read the script she started revealing. That script was evident in the words she repeatedly used and how she played. The pieces of her design began to show a definite pattern. The word "plan" consistently stood out in her dialogue. Her questions almost always centered on that word, "What is the plan?" "Where are we going to sit at the restaurant?" "What will we do?"

In primary grades, my daughter loved school but did not care too much for lunch or recess because there was not a plan. She was obsessed with knowing the plan, understanding it, and being in charge of it. It became very obvious to my wife and me that we had a planner on our hands. "Plan" and "planning" were our daughter's words. If we used them when talking to her, she had the ears to hear us.

It became apparent to us that our job as parents was to affirm what we saw in her. She was testing out who she was, so we wanted to encourage her to believe that what she was doing was a good thing and to see her own design. Therefore, our plan became helping her to understand the "way she should go." Giving her responsibilities at an early age proved to be successful in giving her confidence in her plan. When we saw our daughter not as a blank slate on which to write, but as a script to be read, parenting took on a whole new dimension.

My professional work places me in a position to help leaders with the same thing—understanding their design and their script. To be a good leader, as well as a good parent, we need to make an emotional connection with our followers, including our children. What better way to do that than to know their internal design and help them become confident and self aware, living out their design in a positive way? In short, good leaders help their followers know how their stories fit into His story.

David McKnight

Education: Bethel University, Bethel Seminary, University of Minnesota

Work: Consultant and employee coach for 30 years, best known for unlocking the potential of individuals and organizations by focusing on maximizing giftedness and strengths. Clients include Fortune 500 companies, the United States Army, large and small businesses, and non-profits.

Book: *Failure of Nerve: Leadership in the Age of the Quick Fix* by William H. Friedman

Quote: The best leaders are attuned to themselves and their relationships with others. They understand who they are as leaders, what their strengths and weaknesses are in a role, and how they affect followers. —Robert Kelley, author of *The Power of Followership*

Life is a succession of lessons which must be lived to be understood.
RALPH WALDO EMERSON

Optimism is Catchy

Nancy A. Meyer

On his deathbed, my brother Mark was still trying to get to his son's First Holy Communion ceremony. Mark died of lymphoma two weeks before the event. His optimism and zest for life will always be with me, even decades later.

I remember being three years old and Mark being five. We lived in Bloomington, Minnesota. Mark had never been around the block on his own. One day he ventured out, telling no one.

My mother took me by the hand once she realized Mark was missing. As we hurriedly walked around the corner to the next block, we saw a policeman holding Mark's five-year-old hand. My admiration for his adventurous spirit inspired me to be the entrepreneurial mentor I am today. The risk he took and his enthusiasm to explore was worth the possibility of getting into trouble, he told me later. The life of an entrepreneur—weighing the risks and consequences of following your curiosity—starts early.

I didn't realize until a new United States president took office in January 2017 the importance optimism has played in my life. Optimism replaced fear. This was one of the reasons I joined the Roseville Area Optimist Club in the fall of 2017. I wanted to be around people interested in lifting others up.

I felt I needed more infusions of optimism to counter the negativity delivered worldwide by our tweeting President.

Mary Jo McGuire, a Ramsey County Commissioner, first told me about this club. She encouraged me to join for several months. At the first meeting, I reacquainted myself with a fellow colleague I hadn't seen for several decades, Don Salverda. Don is the founder of our club.

Don reminds me of my brother Mark—positive, upbeat, and always finding a way to bring people together to do great things. Every club member speaks highly of Don. He is admired. He lives, breathes, and role-models the Optimist creed. Don knows everybody by name, and when he introduces table facilitators, he always has wonderful things he remembers about each person. He does the same when he introduces monthly speakers.

I gravitate toward optimistic people like Don and Mary Jo. The culture of the Roseville Area Optimist Club is created from the Optimist creed. Whether we agree or disagree, we have a focal point—our creed. We aren't selling our opinions or trying to convince someone that their opinion has a right or wrong consequence. The creed holds us accountable and gives us permission to come back to being positive, and to keep growing. For example, "Oh, yeah, my health isn't so great but guess what, our creed gives us permission to also focus our conversation on happiness and prosperity. What brings happiness and creates prosperity in your life?" We don't have to wait. We can change the world by bringing optimism into every conversation. The club is our practice ground.

Optimism energizes me and is encouraging. It keeps my life in perspective. When I stumble and fall, optimism helps me look at other possibilities. I am motivated to make greater contributions to our society as a result. Connecting our club activities with youth programs facilitates long-term thinking, fuels mentoring optimism, and promotes inclusion—another club benefit.

Optimism is catchy. People like being around me because the energy of being optimistic brings out the positive energy in them. It feels like a psychological hug. You want more. I am eager to get my psychological hugs every month at the Roseville Area Optimist Club!

Nancy Meyer

Education: B.A., elementary education, Bemidji State University; M.A., special education—certification in emotional development, University of St. Thomas

Work: Founded in 1992 *We*Mentor, inc., an innovative mentoring community where small business owners build seven-figure businesses and become the leaders they envision themselves to be. They reveal who they are as they redesign their business. Podcasts and mindfulness yoga practice are an integral part of the mentoring process.

Book: Three books by Brené Brown, Ph.D., L.M.S.W.: *Daring Greatly; Rising Strong: The Reckoning, The Rumble, The Revolution;* and *Braving The Wilderness: The Quest for True Belonging and the Courage to Stand Alone*

Quote: How wonderful it is that nobody need wait a single moment before starting to improve the world. —Anne Frank

More: www.wementor.com.

Believe

Patrick Miller

This story begins in 2001 while driving down Cicero Avenue in Alsip, Illinois. I saw a business sign on a marquee and at that moment I experience *dé-jà vu*. The moment was very intense. I pulled the car over to the shoulder of the road so I could process what I was feeling. I felt as though I knew what the sign was; that I had seen it before. I felt sure I had been here before, but I had not. I felt a shift in my mind but I could not describe what it was or what I was supposed to do about it. It felt so real I decided to write down on paper the details of what I thought it meant to me.

The main idea that came to me was to start a company and build a brand around my core values, and to use a logo similar to the one that I saw that day. At the time I was so sure that this was it, that I was willing to leave a good company and a great position as a general manager of a supply company—to leave the safety and security of a nice compensation package, paid health care, commissions, company car, and a schedule that I was able to set myself with no oversight. I had a great job and I was willing to leave it because of a thought that turned into a nudge.

At the time I had a two-year-old son and my wife Debra was pregnant with our second child. Nothing about this idea to quit my job and start a company from scratch looked good on paper. We looked closely at the pros and cons. My wife and people with whom I was consulting at the time asked me questions like, "What if this doesn't work out, what are you going to do?" "What is Plan B?" "How are you going to pay for health care for your family?" "Will you be able to pay your mortgage?" "Do you have a well-written business plan?" I was left with a lot of doubt as to whether I could really do this, but my desire to start a company was greater than the risk.

I never graduated from college and I barely graduated from high school. I knew I could sell, and as long as there were people who needed my products or service, I figured I had a job. There is no logic when you are pursuing your passion.

I had a goal: Start a company, and build a culture around my core values that are honesty, integrity, responsibility, and discipline. The logo of the business would remind me that it's not about me—it's about building people; it's about attracting people into the business who share in my core values. It is about giving customers more than what they paid for. It's about building the finest construction company in America. I try to model myself after the finest companies.

On Monday, April 25, 2005, I was sitting at my kitchen table. It was my first day on the job with my newly minted company. My wife was walking down the stairs and stopped half-way down to look at me. I looked up at her and she asked, "What now?" I didn't know what to say as I sat there staring down at the table with a cell phone in front of me. I looked back up at her, pointed to my cell phone, and proclaimed, "I have to find a way to get this thing to ring!"

That first year in business I took an 80% pay cut and was working past 8 p.m. almost every night. My first year in business, I felt like quitting almost every week, but I kept busy and kept moving forward. The only thing I could do to stay motivated was to stay positive and never repeat the negative. The real challenge was to keep a positive mental attitude every day; to persevere through tough problems, issues, adversity, and complete failure.

I've heard it said that the only thing that keeps an entrepreneur going is that they love what they do. I can truly say that for my story, that is true. If I had to work for someone else, and do the same work for (at times) no pay, I am not sure I could have done it. But I was building my company, not someone else's.

On the first project I ever sold, I lost money. I remember driving away with the final payment, which was not enough to cover the labor and materials to complete the project. I remember crying at the wheel while driving home. I remember thinking, "How could this happen?"

I never told the customer my issue, and I didn't ask for more money because the mistake in pricing was my responsibility. I took ownership for my mistake and wrote it off as tuition for a class in the school of hard knocks. Four years later, that same customer came back as a repeat customer and I was awarded my largest contract that year from him. I believe that by keeping my mouth shut, doing more than I was paid for (in this case, a lot more), and keeping a positive mental attitude, the customer came back to me and expected the same service as before.

There is a lot to be said for a positive mental attitude. It is the only thing that doesn't cost me anything and pays *big time*. It's a choice I make every day. It's not a feeling, it's a commitment.

Patrick Miller

Work: Founded Patrick Miller Construction, Inc., in 2005.

Book: *The 7 Habits of Highly Effective People* by Stephen Covey

Quote: Imagination is more important than knowledge. For knowledge is limited, whereas imagination embraces the entire world, stimulating progress, giving birth to evolution.
—Albert Einstein

More: http://pmiller.com/

Many of life's failures are people who did not realize how close they were to success when they gave up.

THOMAS EDISON

My Boss Got It Wrong

Steve Morris

We don't succeed by chance, we succeed by choice. It's a simple saying and yet has such profound truth. In today's world, most people are seduced into the belief that they are born a certain way. Skinny or fat, dumb or smart. The list is endless—all the while discounting the power that daily choices and habits have on our happiness, success and wellbeing.

Let me give you an example. The other day I was on a routine call with my boss. Frankly, I don't even remember what I said or was talking about. However, what my boss said to me stuck with me. "Steve, I think you were just born to be happy. You just have it." What an interesting belief to have.

I find this interesting because I make conscious choices throughout my day to improve my happiness. It's not something I was born with, but rather something I have studied during the past eight years.

Happiness is a subject I take very seriously. I have read more than 60 books in the arena of personal development during the past several years. I have attended seminars, joined civic groups, attended Meetup gatherings and more. My happiness isn't the result of being born under the lucky star, but rather because I took the time to craft it.

Beyond that, I have a daily set of activities to set up the game to win, to "make" me happy. I practice mediation, write in a gratitude journal, work out, practice yoga, take cold showers and eat healthfully. Mind you, these all are learned habits. I grew up in a house that didn't partake in half these daily disciplines.

I am not going to argue that genetics don't have a role in happiness, because they certainly do. What I am here to say is that our choices and daily lifestyle habits often trump genetics. Am I perfect? Absolutely not, but I strive each and every day to be the best version of me. And that makes me happy.

Education: B.A., communications, Minnesota State-Mankato

Work: Current: senior account executive, SAP, one year. Application sales representative, Oracle Corp., four years.

Book: *Millionaire Fastlane* by M.J. DeMarco

Quote: Shallow men believe in luck. Strong men believe in cause and effect. —Ralph Waldo Emerson

More: www.linkedin.com/in/steve-morris-630b582b

I Have a Calling. So Should You.

Mark Nagel

When I was in high school, I was not a good student and was told by several guidance counselors that I should not go to college but should attend a vocational school. I had no aptitude for carpentry or automotive mechanics, nor any desire to pursue those career paths. As Bill Jensen said in his book, *Simplicity: The New Competitive Advantage*, "In a world of infinite choices, it's hard to make a decision." But I had to. In order to be accepted at the University of Delaware, I had to earn B's in two college-level classes. And after that, I needed to choose a major.

After much reading and reflection, I came up with three things that were necessary for a rewarding "calling"—find something you love to do all the time, make sure that you're good at it, and, of course, make sure it's something that people will pay you to do. Simple enough, right? What I mean here is that I didn't want a "position" where the work was just a "means to an end," an 8 to 4:30 job or a "career" that simply meant "moving up the ladder" in a position in which I did not love the work. I wanted a "calling," something that helped people, provided challenge, and where I could make a difference in some small way. Gandhi once said, "Be the change you want to see in the world" which is what I've tried to do over the past 40 years.

As Wade Walcutt said in his article, "I Get It—Why We Have the Greatest Jobs in the World" in *Parks and Recreation Business* magazine, we should never lose sight of why we do the work we do in the first place, so I begin each day with why I do what I do.

Every day I get to:
· Build a better community
· Engage people one-on-one on civic projects
· Work with people who share a common purpose and are committed to making a difference
· Be energized through meeting diverse people with different ideas and perspectives
· Be part of something bigger than myself or any one person
· Learn new information and meet new challenges
· Be inspired by others
· Mentor the next generation

I have found a calling and my hope is that everyone finds one. When you do, as Coach John Wooden once said, "You'll have both a positive attitude and peace of mind." My motto is, "No need to retire, continue to inspire."

One final note is that I read books that reinforce this calling. Right now, I'm reading the *Power of Purpose—Find Meaning, Live Longer, Better* by local author, Richard J. Leider, which is a good place to start your journey on your calling.

Mark Nagel

Education: B.A.A.S., sociology major, economics minor, University of Delaware; M.P.A., urban administration and finance, The Ohio State University; M.B.A., finance, University of St. Thomas

Work: For nearly 40 years, I have been a local government manager with 15 years as a community college professor of business. I own my own consulting business and invest in startup companies.

Book: *The Power of Purpose: Find Meaning, Live Longer, Better* by local author, Richard J. Leider

There is neither good or bad, but thinking makes it so.
WILLIAM SHAKESPEARE

Shaped by God's Hand

Ralph Olsen

I grew up on the north side of Chicago. Our family lived in a garden apartment, which meant we lived in the basement and our windows were at ground level. As a young boy, I would stand on the couch, look out the window and watch the feet walk by every day. When I asked my mother where the feet were going, she would say, "Oh, someday you'll know."

My mother was a person who had unique expressions on life. My favorite expression of hers was, "I trust you as far as I can see it." I wasn't quite sure what that meant, but I learned it wasn't so crazy after all, for it meant whenever I left home I was responsible for my actions. Trust is built by living your life being true to what you say and do.

My father was a factory worker who quit school in 10th grade because school was boring. He worked hard and after work he would go to the Chug-A-Lug, the neighborhood bar, to drink with his friends. Family life was not easy. I learned that my grandfather, my father, my uncle and two male cousins were all alcoholics—and all dropped out of school before graduating. I realized this was not the life I wanted. I was going to graduate high school and go to college.

My Grandma Daisy always told me that God had an amazing plan for my life. All I had to do was trust Him, place my hand in His and I would have an amazing life. A quote that has inspired me in my life journey is found in the words of Mahatma Gandhi, "We must become the change we wish to see in the world." So, I am the first high school, college and seminary graduate in my family. I am, also, the first non-alcoholic male in my family.

As I began to look at colleges, my high school guidance counselor told me "You have decent grades, but I would look at a state college because private colleges take 'the cream of the crop.'" My choir teacher said, "You have a good voice, but I wouldn't count on making the top choir in college—but keep singing." Well, I was accepted to a private college, auditioned and made the top-touring choir as a freshman, and though it wasn't always easy, I was blessed with caring teachers and received a B.A. degree in English from Augustana College in Illinois.

In the summers during college, my pastor would encourage me to consider the ministry. After college graduation, with some strong encouragement from my pastor—some might have called it arm-twisting—I enrolled at Luther Seminary in St. Paul. Four years later, I received my master of divinity degree and have served in pastoral ministry for forty-three years. Grandma Daisy was right—God did have an amazing plan for my life.

From humble beginnings in that "garden apartment" to places near and far, and with God's amazing blessing, I have sought to "walk the talk" with compassion, enthusiasm and integrity following the words of the prophet Micah 6:8, "What does the Lord require of you but to do justice, and to love kindness and to walk humbly with your God."

Ralph Olsen

Education: B.A., English and commu-nications, Augustana College, Rock Island, IL; Master of Divinity, pastoral ministry, Luther Seminary, St. Paul, MN

Work: Interim pastor, Trinity Lutheran, Hammond, WI, 2016-present; devel-opment officer, Union Gospel Mission, St. Paul, 2011-2014; founder/senior pastor, King of Kings Lutheran Church, Woodbury, MN, 1980-2010; associate pastor, Augustana Lutheran, West St. Paul, 1975-1980. • Author of *Shaped by God's Hand* in 2013.

Book: *The Trust Edge* by David Horsager, *Choosing Civility* by P.M. Forni, and *Audacity* by Jonathan Chait

Quote: There can be no keener revelation of a society's soul than the way in which it treats its children. —Nelson Mandela

While we may not be able to control all that happens to us, we can control what happens inside us.

DR. MARTIN LUTHER KING JR.

Pilot in Command

Scott Plum

Since I was 11 years old, I have wanted to be a pilot. Unfortunately, I was told I could never achieve that goal because my eyes are so bad. Though the barrier was not true, I maintained that belief until the fall of 1996. At the age of 30, I decided I was no longer going to subscribe to that belief. It was real, but no longer true.

The very first day of class, the flight instructor stood in front of the entire class and said, "As a pilot, you are the PIC—Pilot-In-Command—which means you are 100% responsible for the safety and operations of this aircraft at all times. If anything ever goes wrong, you cannot blame the weather, another pilot, the tower, or the aircraft manufacturer. *You* are responsible for everything you do and don't do."

WOW, I thought. For the first time in my life, I felt I was 100% personally accountable for every one of my actions. If I blamed others for my failures and misfortunes, there was no reason for me to change, because it's not my fault. However, when I own every outcome and take responsibility for it, if I don't receive the results I want, I'm the only one who can make a difference in the future.

This outlook is a choice, and one that only I can make and maintain.

Having an outlook of optimism is a choice, which will be tested every day. You are the PIC in your life. You are the only one who can change your results. And this will take commitment.

When you commit to a task, project, or decision, your persistence will increase the likelihood of a favorable outcome. Here are examples of how your commitment can be applied:

Success is possible only when you have a greater commitment to achieve the goal than the consequences you will experience if you fail. Do you know the consequences if you fail? Are you willing to accept them? If you cannot live with them, your commitment is the means of overcoming them.

Commitment means you are living up to your true potential. It is sad to hear someone say to another that they have potential. The person hearing that remark does not have enough confidence and commitment in themselves to apply their gifts. Others see their gifts, but they are not shared for one reason or another.

What are you willing to tolerate in your life?

Do you accept poor results? Are you expecting others to accept low standards? Success will not arrive if you don't expect it. Commitment means you will set a high standard. Encourage others to raise their standards. Deliver only high standards, and look back at your followers as you take the lead.

How do you show your commitment to others? Is commitment a word others would use to describe you? Build a reputation of commitment. It's your choice—a decision only you can make and maintain.

Scott Plum

Work: Founder of the Minnesota Sales Institute with more than 30 years of experience in training, workshops, classes, and one-on-one coaching and consulting. • Author of the book titled *Taking Off Into the Wind* that continues to inspire others on overcoming adversity and applying their commitment.

Book: *The Magic of Thinking Big* by David Schwartz, Ph.D.

Quote: It is better to take refuge in the Lord than to trust in man. —Psalms 118:8

More: www.mnsales.com.

The capacity for hope is the most significant fact of life. It provides human beings with a sense of destination and the energy to get started

NORMAN COUSINS

What Exactly Do *You* Stand For?

Dan Prosser

With so much vitriol in the world today, it's a wonder that optimism actually can find a place in our culture and institutions. With so much energy directed at being against the things that upset many of us, it's perhaps time to pose the question: "What are you *for*?" It takes so much energy and a great loss of power to be in a conversation against something or against others—without knowing what in fact you stand *for*.

Has being "against" something really ever contributed positively to us as a nation, or in our families or our communities?

At the time of this writing (January 2018), we celebrate the 89th birthday of an extraordinarily great man, Dr. Martin Luther King Jr. We need to ask, "Was the civil rights movement he led *against* discrimination or *for* equality for everyone?" Yes, there were Americans who objected and protested against the way they were being treated by other Americans. Yet, we are reminded that Martin Luther King stood fast in painting a picture of what could be—a future with miraculous possibility in the face of some of the most inhuman treatment I've ever witnessed in my life. King was assassinated 50 years ago this year, at the age of 39.

Most Americans are familiar with King's iconic August 28, 1963 "I Have a Dream" speech, addressing a crowd at the March on Washington for Jobs and Freedom. From the steps of the Lincoln Memorial, eight times he referred to his theme "I Have A Dream." It was a dream *for* a better future—*for* all people, not just people of color. He spoke a language that we can still understand today—that to dream is being *for* something.

King said it. He was *for* "…the riches of freedom and the security of [racial] justice," and "brotherhood." He didn't put anyone down or make anyone wrong to declare it. He spoke like a true optimist. Yet, he also pointed to a clear and present danger, and had us see that America was headed in the wrong direction— -and it was. Yet, many people in powerful positions in government at that time feared what a powerful black civil rights leader could create by speaking to the people who were victimized by despicable treatment by others.

And what did threatened people do with that stand? They vilified King and called him a subversive. One thing, though, is clear and true for me: Martin Luther King made a difference with more people because he had the vision and foresight to share a dream *for* something possible and positive. Just read a version of his speech and it can bring tears to your eyes when you get present to the amazing possibility of this man's vision and what, even today, he still shows us is possible—the seemingly impossible.

Those who know, know that Martin Luther King was not against *any* others. He was not against you or me. The power of his movement, that still lives on today, lives on because it was *for* something. And what he was *for* was a more powerful conversation than being against. He was *for* bringing all people together—black and white—in a way that made sense for the masses.

The more people fought, the slower the change. Whenever there is a fight or anger, people don't feel safe, and when they don't feel safe, they won't get on board. Most of us cannot possibly imagine what it was like in the middle of the last century, and what people did to other human beings—in America even. The only way that was possible was for some people to see others as not being human, and to dehumanize them. So, I ask you...

What are *you* for?

This is why I contemplate, for example, whether the women's march against President Trump will have the momentum to be sustainable. I don't know. The march captured a limiting and fixed mindset of people who listened to their emotions and claims of victimization after Trump was sworn in as president.

Then there was the March for Life the very following week that has now celebrated its 45th consecutive year. Imagine what can be done in a movement that stands *for* something? Something clear and focused; something everyone can get behind. Something like life.

What's the message for those of us in business, and especially for optimists? This needs to translate.

So-called "movements" *against* anything always need to create the pretense of being something they're not, to appear as if they are successful. But, they're not *for* anything. They're narrowly focused *against*, and the positivity of being *for* always overcomes the negativity of being *against*.

When you use the power of a little three-letter word—*for*—to change the conversation, I believe you gain the power to transform the way the world works (at the very least, the reality of your own world). So, ultimately, to be *for* something is about gaining your power in relationship to your desire to achieve great things.

You can't possibly know what you're against if you don't first confront what you are *for*. And most recently, so many people literally don't really know what they are so angry about except that the person they believed was entitled to win an election…did not.

And therein lies the problem. People with entitlement mentality, who feel their emotions count for something and that others should listen to them, rarely listen to what others are saying. Those who feel entitled miss the opportunity to understand what is happening—topics that others might be pointing to, such as Martin Luther King did that day in August 1963. I was alive. I heard it. I was perhaps too young to truly understand it then. But I knew King's speech was about greatness, and I can understand it today.

And, what King's message says to me is that some will try to appeal to our emotions for good, and some will try to stir up trouble because they feel threatened and want *you* to fight their fight for them.

When you're against something or someone, you generate negativity—anger even. As far as I know, anger is not a positive feeling. Focusing on anger will get you more of what you don't want—more anger and greater anger. And ultimately you will lose your power to make real positive, lasting change—if that's what you truly want.

Remember, your thoughts become the very things you spend your time thinking about, and the path to what you really want gets tougher than it has to be if it's not *for* good. If you want a change in government and you think what you propose has value, bring it. But bring it in a way that others can hear you and get on board, not because they are angry but because they, too, are *for* a better way of life that a possibility can usher in for all mankind—not just a few angry souls.

Go ahead and tell me—tell us—what do you stand *for* today?

Dan Prosser

Work: Launched four companies. Mentoring CEOs and their teams. Speaker, SaaS software developer, and the best-selling author of *Thirteeners: Why Only 13 Percent of Companies Successfully Execute Their Strategy and How Yours Can Be One of Them.*

Book: *The Disappearance of the Universe* by Gary R. Renard

Quote: If you don't like something, change it. If you can't change it, change your attitude. —Maya Angelou

More: http://www.danprosser.com/
https://www.linkedin.com/in/dprosser/

Only in the darkness can you see the stars.

DR. MARTIN LUTHER KING JR.

If It Is To Be, It Is Up To Me

Ted Risdall

My grandmother gave me a rock as a birthday gift! On the rock was inscribed all two-letter words that said, "If it is to be, it is up to me."

On my next birthday, I got a rock that said, "Believe in yourself."

On yet another birthday, another rock that said, "Never give up."

My grandmother was an incredibly accomplished woman for her generation. She could drive, she worked hard, saved money, and bought her own Baskin Robbins ice cream chain where she employed her four boys. She started book clubs, garden clubs, and formed the Rock Garden Society. She went back to school and became a master gardener.

My grandmother is someone I look up to for her incredible will power, can-do attitude, and ability to lead and inspire others.

We were best of friends.

These rocks have become part of my life and determination to make a difference every day. In life, moving any rock can be a challenge and sometimes the small ones are harder than the big ones.

My son came home and said he had a job interview at 3M in the R&D lab to work on artificial intelligence. I said, "Congratulations, that is exactly what you want to do."

He said, "But I am petrified. What if I fail? What if I cannot do the job? What if I cannot solve the problems? Maybe I should wait and get more experience doing something else."

I smiled and said, "Let me go get my box of rocks."

He said, "I do not understand," and I said, "Wait, you'll see."

I grabbed my box of rocks and said, "I have a great gift for you. Here are your rocks. Please, go accept the job, and bring these rocks with you each day."

Remember:

"Believe in yourself."

"If it is to be, it is up to me."

"Never give up."

Go find some rocks and paint these words on them. Carry them always.

Ted Risdall

Education: B.S., business administration, USIU, San Diego; M.B.A. Thunderbird School of Global Management, Arizona State University

Work: CEO Risdall Marketing Group, LLC, for the past 31 years.

Book: *The Untethered Soul* by Michael Singer

Quote: The reasonable man adapts himself to the world: the unreasonable one persists in trying to adapt the world to himself. Therefore all progress depends on the unreasonable man. —George Bernard Shaw, *Man and Superman*

More: https://www.risdall.com/

Embracing My Personal Miracle

Patty Sagert

I consider myself a curious eternal optimist by nature. Growing up, my mom instilled this phrase in my siblings and me, "If you run with the dogs, you get the fleas." This phrase seems very straightforward and easy to comprehend on the surface level. As I moved into adulthood, I have had more time to reflect on this phrase and how I apply it to my life. I see this phrase applying to the people with whom I choose to surround myself and also to my thoughts and behaviors. This concept and thought alignment became clearer for me as I aged and experienced some life-altering challenges.

In 2010, I experienced a challenge that put the phrase into perspective for me. I was studying and completing my Master of Arts degree at Gonzaga University. As one of my electives, I opted to take a class at Saint Andrew's Abbey located in Valyermo, California, in the Mojave Desert. The subject and focus of the course was community. As a participant, I was given very little information about what to expect from this experience. To prepare, students were asked to read the Rules of St. Benedict. (St. Andrew's Abbey is a monastic community filled with male Benedictine monks and oblates.)

I had a sense of unease and fear going into the experience as I didn't know what to expect. Frankly, I worried about the time I would have to spend in complete silence with myself and my thoughts. I was a person who always craved stimulation through conversations, activity, music or television playing in the background, distracting me every moment of my waking day.

As students, we followed the monks day-to-day flow, getting up before dawn for prayer services in their chapel, eating with them, working with them, learning from them and ending the day in silence, prayer and contemplation. A portion of every morning was spent in Lectio Divina (Latin for "divine reading")—quiet, focused scriptural reading, meditation and prayers. The week was capped with time to interview some of the monks to learn their back stories, and a feast of celebration for one of the monk's birthdays. The richness of this experience left a meaningful impact on my life.

Leaving the monastery and heading back to blustery Minnesota, I promised myself that I would incorporate some of my key learns into my life. This was put to the test shortly after my return from Saint Andrew's Abbey. I began to feel ill. I spent a week at home and could not seem to shake a high-grade fever and what appeared to be the worst flu symptoms imaginable. I ended up at the emergency room, getting admitted into the hospital. After the first night, I was rushed up to the ICU. The infectious disease doctors and the rest of the team could not figure out what was causing my illness. They sent vial after vial of blood to the Mayo Clinic to the point of my arms turning black and blue from all of the blood draws.

I ended up spending several days on a ventilator, fighting for my life. I was scared and desperate to have the doctors uncover and name my illness. All in all, I spent 12 days in the hospital with the doctors unable to determine the cause of my illness. The infectious-disease doctors said that there were only two options left—cancer or leukemia. They could not determine the cause of the illness or the miracle that was to be my full recovery. I firmly believe that my miracle was a combination of great medical care, the power of prayer (I had monks in two monasteries praying for me along with my faith community, family and friends), and also the power of positivity and optimism. Not once did I feel sorry for myself or my condition. I embraced the lessons I learned at Saint Andrew's Abbey, allowing myself to find comfort in my recovery, especially during the quiet nights spent in the ICU, trying to regain my strength and stamina.

This journey has led me to embrace the power of optimism and faith. I am blessed beyond measure. The Roseville Area Optimist Club has given me a community of positive, like-minded people who share my commitment to choose positivity, joy and optimism to influence and impact the world around us.

Patty Sagert

Education: B.A., marketing and management, Metropolitan State University; M.A., organizational leadership with a certificate in servant-leadership from Gonzaga University

Work: Campus director at Rasmussen College in Blaine, MN, 11 years. Previously in the insurance industry.

Book: *Educated* by Tara Westover.

Quote: Be true to your work, your word, and your friend. —Henry David Thoreau

More: Facebook and LinkedIn

Life is About Lessons

Mark E. Smith

As a young boy, I was blessed to have the opportunity to spend my summers in a small town in Upper Peninsula of Michigan. Many of my aunts were teachers and they all traveled "home" from various cities to be together for the summer. Therefore, I got the chance to spend extended time with my grandparents, cousins and other family members. We all piled into our grandparent's house and had a wonderful time together. For me, it became a great life lesson to learn how to respect others, contribute to the family, develop patience and appreciate each other's talents. Living in a small town also gave me insight on the different values people have in a less economically sound area compared to a big city. No one cared what brand of bike or fishing pole you had; they would just stop by the house and off you went to the next adventure together. It was refreshing to not continually compare yourself to others and just enjoy doing stuff with friends.

My grandfather was a great mentor. He grew up working in a lumber camp and never really had time to be a kid. I believe he lived his childhood vicariously through me. We spent a lot of time together and he taught me how to appreciate nature. He helped me learn that I did not have to be afraid of the forest, how to listen, to think logically and to navigate in the trees. That perspective has led me to countless hours of exploring and enjoyment. In return, he let me teach him how to fish. To this day, I do not know if he knew how or if he was just giving me a growth experience of teaching an adult something new. It did give me a great deal of satisfaction and pride to share that with him.

My grandfather was also a member of the Masonic Lodge. He lived their values, and he taught me the importance of treating every person with respect. We spent many days together visiting old men, bringing them meals, helping with projects and listening to the stories of their lives. At the time, I never really understood why we did it but now can appreciate his kind nature and dedication to helping people in need.

I was fortunate to grow up with supportive and loving parents. My father was a mechanical engineer and was constantly teaching me how things work. He gave me a perspective to be inquisitive and look at things from a basic functional level. He would take something apart, with the philosophy of, "What is the worst thing that can happen? It is already broken."

Developing new skills brought me confidence and has saved me a significant amount of money over the years. In his career, my dad had to continually learn new skills or run the risk of getting outdated. He taught me the need to continually bring value to the company you work for, and that you have the responsibility of maintaining your own education.

In addition, my dad fostered my love of sports. He made time to help me develop my skills in the backyard. He taught me the importance of being a good teammate, to understand you get out what you put in and to take personal responsibility for your playing time. He also explained that there are times when you are the best and times when others are just more talented. That is life, but if you enjoy something, do not quit but instead do your best. Control the things you can and accept the results.

My mother taught me many things. As a school librarian, she saw many different students every day and reminded us all that each person has a different story. Be kind to all people because everyone has a unique situation and you might be the most positive part of their day. Be understanding and do not judge others for things out of their control. My mother was always there for me and never missed one of my games. It was always comforting to have that support whether I played or not.

One of the most influential things my parents did for us was travel. We planned road trips as a family and saved for vacations years away. The trips gave us something to look forward to and gave us a bigger perspective of the world. Lessons of budget planning, sacrifice (needs vs. wants) and the anticipation to experience new things have been valuable ideals throughout my life.

There was never a doubt that I was going to college to further my education. My parents always taught us to plan for the future and foresee the path we were going to take. They let us choose our own direction but always asked probing questions to ensure we considered important aspects of that path. They helped us financially but made sure we paid for a significant portion of our education. It was an investment in bettering ourselves. They never once asked about my grades because that was my responsibility to myself, and it did not matter to anyone else because it was my future I was working toward. In reflecting back, I see how they were instilling responsibility and self-motivation in my actions.

When I began my working career, I focused on bringing

value to my employer and viewed my job as though they were investing in my skills. I never understood some of my co-workers who worked by the clock and complained about their pay rate per hour. It was eye opening to see the amount of time they wasted, the unwillingness to do things outside of their job responsibilities and the closed view they had of their employment. At that time, I made the conscious choice not to take that path, to disassociate with that mindset and learn new skills every day. It was amazing the opportunities that opened up to me and how I advanced through the organization.

Another important insight was talking to my college class-mates. Only seven of 29 students were working in their intended field of study. Most complained about a lack of opportunity, but I realized it was mostly a lack of planning on their part. This thought instilled in me that there are many people available in the workforce and I need to continue to focus on bringing value to my employer.

As I became more involved with the leadership of the orga-nization, it has been invaluable to have worked in most aspects of our operation. To fully appreciate what staff does, to know what they deal with on a daily basis and the skills necessary has assisted me in making sound organizational decisions. Leadership needs to get their hands dirty, listen and contin-ually touch base with all of their employees. This interaction helps staff understand where their leadership is coming from and why decisions are made. The creation of mutual respect and open understanding is a key to effectively carrying out the organizational vision and goals.

Mentoring is a part of the job I truly enjoy. When I reflect back on my early days, I have such an appreciation for those who helped me learn new skills. Therefore, I strive to encourage others in their personal development and to become a positive part of their working careers. It gives me great satisfaction to know I helped someone develop new skills, readjust their mindset, advance their position or just better themselves.

I have taken advantage of educational opportunities available in my organization. At local universities, I pursued additional business coursework and obtained certificates in public administration and various technical skills. Through conducting training sessions, I have improved my public speaking for local, regional and national meetings. Through managing projects, I have improved my organizational skills, meeting deadlines and communication skills. While partnering with manufacturers, I have strived to understand their business objectives to develop win/win agreements and maintain beneficial long-term relationships. When given the possibility to educate legislators in Washington, D.C., I ventured into a new arena and received another perspective of government operations. A valuable lesson is the mentality you take when you fulfill your responsibilities. It is either a task or an opportunity to improve yourself; the choice is yours.

My employer has supported my personal development. Opportunities to attend effective management courses, leadership growth groups, seminars, and regional and national meetings continue to grant me new insights that I can bring into our organization. It is important to note, a person has to seek their own occasions in which to grow and they should not wait passively for someone to give them the chance. Pursue opportunities or they may never come.

When my wife and I moved our growing family to a small town in western Wisconsin, we made the choice to become an active part of our community. Many outlying towns can become bedroom communities and many new residents fail to recognize the history, traditions and values of the area. This lack of understanding can create rifts in these developing communities when no assimilation occurs. The leadership of this community had tremendous foresight and made the choice not to give up their small-town identity when the new bridge was built over the St Croix River.

In the year 2000, our community leaders started the Front Porch Project in which citizens were encouraged to meet and engage with their neighbors. People were welcomed to civic events and to participate in community decisions. In order to promote positive interaction, community leaders created a program called the "Leadership Trust Initiative" in which community members could develop leadership skills, understand the history of the town, get to know current leaders, listen to new community members and learn methods of positive discourse.

The program intertwined lifelong community members with new residents and has been a great success. I participated early in the curriculum and became part of the steering committee. I am proud to say we have had ten different groups go through the six-month training course since 2006. We have high community engagement in our city's decisions and I have seen citizen's use of these leadership skills on church councils, sports association boards, in public meetings and the like. Many great lessons have been learned from this experience. The importance of a clear vision, communicating the importance of community needs, uniting like-minded people and empowering the individual to make a difference were all of tremendous value.

Since we would be raising our family in this town, we want this community to be a place that our children would be proud to call their home and have a sense of belonging. It is my hope that they will believe that each of us can benefit the greater good and make a positive difference at the local level. I have already seen each of them take various leadership roles in school activities, with community events, on sport teams, at church and with various charities. They have gravitated toward these roles on their own initiative, but it makes me proud to see them grow and step out of their comfort zones to lead others.

I have served on sports association boards and coached multiple sports for many years. Coaching youth sports can be extremely rewarding and extremely frustrating at times. The enjoyable aspects are seeing youth continually improve, gain confidence and bond with teammates while working toward a common goal.

I have been fortunate to be associated with more team success than failure. To help players develop that mentality to compete at the best of their ability and to celebrate the success of others will hopefully stick with them. As they age, coaching teenagers gets to be a challenging adventure. Unfortunately, many parents start to believe the coaches are impeding their child's path to a Division 1 scholarship. Important lessons gained from this experience are to focus on the reason you are there (the kids), to reward effort, to continue to learn and evolve, to understand that you cannot please everyone and to be candid in your communication.

My greatest life experience was meeting my wife. She is the most optimistic and caring person that I know. She is a beautiful person inside and out, and she inspires me on many levels. I am so fortunate to have her in my life. I learn new things every day about the importance of family, love, faith, friendships, gratitude, supporting other's goals and striving each day to be a better person. I am always amazed how taking a single risk to ask out a pretty girl could put me on a path of such a wonderful life!

Optimism has played a major role in my life. My life has been filled with tremendous mentors and positive examples that I have used to base my decisions. I often reflect on all of these experiences and am eternally grateful for having these opportunities. It is my hope that someday someone will be able to look back at my life and believe I was a positive influence on them.

Mark E. Smith

Education: B.S., biological science, chemistry minor, University of Minnesota; accounting and purchasing, Metro State University; certificate in public administration, Hamline University

Work: Purchasing manager and technical services, Metropolitan Mosquito Control District; analyst, Minnesota Agricultural Aircraft Association; entomological consultant, Minnesota Pollution Control Agency. Past president/treasurer, North Central Mosquito Control Association, Vector-Borne Disease Advisory Board, Bayer Corporation. Leadership Trust Initiative steering committee, City of New Richmond, WI.

Book: *True North* by Bill George

Quote: I hope I shall possess firmness and virtue enough to maintain what I consider the most enviable of all titles, the character of an honest man. —George Washington

Don't Buy Cheap Toilet Paper

Curt Stockford

I have found the challenge to offer a gem of useful advice surprisingly difficult. In considering what value I might add to another's understanding of how to create a successful life, I find myself instead thinking of advice offered by a handful of others.

"To thine own self be true," says Polonius in Shakespeare's *Hamlet*. That advice worked for me five-plus decades ago in a senior class address. I believed it then. I believe it still, and now more fully understand it. Though it continues to stand me in good stead, it seems more of a building block of personal values than a practical bit of advice.

"Measure twice; cut once." This is a proverb that served me well as a carpenter for more than four decades. Great advice, but somewhat limited in the extent of its audience.

And, so, in the search for some bit of wisdom that is useful, practical, original and nearly universal, it occurs to me that, "Don't buy cheap toilet paper" fills that bill. I believe that with some consideration and personal experience, most will find this advice to be of sound value.

Alright, I admit to some attempt at irony in this last scrap of advice. My hope, however, is that it illustrates how difficult it is to offer meaningful advice to others, especially if one's target audience is considerably younger. I make this judgment based solely on my personal experience. I ask myself, "What advice would I or did I accept?' in my youth and beyond. The honest answer is "Not much." Of that which I accepted, how much did I incorporate into daily life? Again, the answer must be, "Not much." So, what have I learned from this self-evaluation? Ahh, now we're getting somewhere. I have found what generations of others have already discovered, namely that life is full of challenges, that life is not always fair, that honesty with both others and yourself is the best policy, that your attitude can be your greatest asset, and that kindness matters. So, there's a basket of awareness that each of us is destined to discover for ourselves … if we're lucky.

As profound as these realizations may be, they do not rise to the status of advice, however. Again, I ask myself, what can I contribute to the personal or collective knowledge that will be useful to others in navigating the realities of life?

Certainly, nothing I share will prevent the difficulties or unfairness that you will at times encounter. No wisdom will alleviate the pain suffered through personal loss, betrayal, or dashed expectations of your fellow man. There is, however, one thing that anchors me during times of both joy and adversity. And, that is the awareness of **purpose** for my life. Here's how it works. Once discovered, **purpose** enables you to develop a **vision** of where your life is headed. Having a **vision**—a big concept—makes navigating the challenges encountered many times easier. Your focus will remain on the ultimate result and not the immediate obstacle to it. This may seem simplistic, but I guarantee that discovering your purpose and creating a vision for yourself will benefit you in countless ways.

So, what is purpose? How will you find it? How will you know when you have it? Admittedly, these are big questions, especially since the answers will likely be different for everyone.

And, did I mention that your purpose will probably change with the stages of your life? Let me explain.

First, we have to understand purpose. Hundreds, perhaps thousands, of books have been written that define and deal with purpose in life. I have nothing to add. I define purpose simply as an understanding of your reason for being. It need not be grand, ethereal, or forever. In fact, a purpose during your teens might be as simple as moving through adolescence and embarking on the road to an independent life, education, job, and relationships. As a young adult, especially one in a committed relationship with another, your purpose may very well be to create and care for a family. This may be a decades-long purpose and responsibility, one that consumes the majority of your time and energy.

At a later stage in life you may have the freedom to consider purpose based less upon practical realities and more upon philosophies and values. Redefining purpose at this point in your life may well offer avenues of pursuit and personal fulfillment of which you had never dared dream. As wonderful as this can be, it does not diminish the importance of the very practical purposes in earlier stages of your life.

Furthermore, purpose is not always a matter of search and discovery. Many have grown up in the arms of a church or religious ideology that encourages a life that is led according to principles of humanity and personal giving. Most spiritual beliefs, even those lacking a disciplined structure, lead us on a path that challenges us to determine our greater reason for being, our purpose. Indeed, even those without any of these affiliations will no doubt come to believe in the tenets of humanity, respect, and mutual aid. Such values are essential to our survival within groups. All of these can be the foundation of a purpose for our life.

How will you discover your purpose? The path of discovery will differ for each, but here are a few suggestions. Read. Joseph Addison said, "Reading is to the mind what exercise is to the body." Great ideas and inspiration await you with the turning of a page. Learn what others already know.

Associate with purposeful people. To quote Jim Rohn, "You are the average of the five people you spend the most time with." Look around you. Who do you admire for their attitude, their positive effect, and their productivity? Become part of their universe. They will expand your perspective and open new possibilities in you.

Pursue positivity with a vengeance. Negative thoughts and attitudes victimize you. They limit your joy in daily living and your opportunities for personal growth. A positive attitude is simply a choice that you make on the way in which you will view any situation. Positivity is a discipline that you can learn. It will open doors not even visible to those with a negative perspective.

Change your vocabulary. We all apply different connotations to the same words, but here are a few that might be worth reconsidering. Exchange "problem" for "challenge" or even "opportunity." Consider "criticism" to be "feedback." Try changing "should" to "could" and "have to" to "choose to." Not only will the listener interpret your message differently; you may also find that your perspective in dealing with the message has become more positive as well.

How will you know when you have found your purpose? This is the most subjective of the questions regarding purpose. I unapologetically offer you the vaguest of answers. It's like love. You'll know it when you see it. I believe that the self-discovery of purpose affords in us a sense of peacefulness, a self-assuredness, and a quiet joy in the activities that fulfill that purpose. I also believe that it's impossible to hide the effects of a purposeful life from those around us. Even without tangible measurement, those in our proximity sense it in us.

And, so, I hope that I have made the case for the pursuit of purpose in your life. As mentioned, there is not a one-size-fits-all formula for either the timing or type of purpose. Neither is it a static life asset, one that once claimed you will forever possess. The value of understanding your purpose is nearly without measure, because it pervades all parts of your life. It offers you broad personal horizons, provides a fuller perspective on your world, and affords a pathway of satisfying activities. This in turn makes you a more valuable partner, friend, and associate, no matter how large or small your personal universe.

My wish for you is that you continually search for and evaluate your purpose. The process will be not just instructional, but at times exhilarating. And, remember, when all profound advice has been exhausted, "Don't buy cheap toilet paper" will still be of value.

Curt Stockford

Education: R.W. Traip Academy

Work: Residential remodeling contractor (retired).

Book: *Life's Greatest Lessons* by Hal Urban

Quote: This above all: to thine own self be true, and it must follow, as night the day, Thou cans't not then be false to any man. —William Shakespeare (*Hamlet*)

Cranking the Flywheel

David Swan

My grandpa, born in 1895, was a farmer who survived (barely) the depression. The fondest memories of my youth were spent with Grandpa—working with horses, planting the garden, woodworking and farming. In the late '70s when I was entering my teen years, my grandpa and I would frequent the farm of my great uncle and help him out for endless hours every summer. Uncle George was a bachelor and an interesting fellow. Spending time on his farm was literally like going back in time. His new machinery was from 1930, but most was much older. George still milked cows by hand and used archaic farming techniques.

Whether Grandpa and I were getting grain to feed the cows and horses or bagging up oats for planting in the spring, the prerequisite task was always the same—using the dreaded fanning mill. A fanning mill, also known as a threshing wheel or grain separator, is a hand-cranked wood box about the size of a washing machine. This process is done today with huge modern combines. In the late 1800s, you used the fanning mill, a time-consuming, laborious process.

Grandpa would pour the dusty grain in the top of the box and I would crank a large, metal handle that probably could have used a gallon of grease to help it move. As a kid, it took all my power to turn that crank. My efforts would rotate a

236

large cylindrical fan that would blow the grain seed through a series of screens. The end result was that the dirt, weed seeds, chaff, pebbles, straw, dust and rat crap would be separated and blow out a shoot, leaving pure grain seed that would fall in our bucket. The process was messy, incredibly dusty and a nasty, nasty job. It was fun for 10 seconds, and then miserable for the next ten minutes…all for just one pail of grain.

What sense did this make? Certainly if the cows and horses were hungry enough, they could sort through the dust, stones and weed seeds and eat what they wanted. When planting fields, we could just raise the application rate on the steel-wheeled planter by 40% and get the same yield, right?

I went to that shed with my grandpa a couple hundred times. And although I cherished my time with Grandpa, I would always ask (whine), "Grandpa, why do we have to do this?"

Sometimes, Grandpa would just smile and keep pouring grain in the mill so I had to keep cranking. But, when he did answer, his response was the same. "David, because when we are done with this nasty job, we are 100% certain that what we have remaining is very pure, very clean and exactly what we want. The messy and hard jobs in life that no one wants to do are the most important."

In life, you need to do some threshing, and very, very few people want to crank the handle and get really dusty. We prefer to take the seed we have and hope all will work out rather than perform difficult tasks to ensure that our product, life or relationships are the best they can be. It is easier to not have tough conversations…not venture into complete honesty. It is much simpler to cut corners and focus on the "fun" part of our jobs than to work on boring details, confront issues and do less-rewarding tasks that are the most important.

So why do the work? Why get dirty? Why not just "think positive" about the cards we have been dealt—the grain in the shed? Because we have the power to do more. To be more. To give more. The nasty dust and weed seed that never gets pushed out of the flywheel is what hinders us from forming relationships, building teams, raising kids and accomplishing things that are truly special. Really Special.

Opening your soul to others is hard; it is much simpler to keep much hidden. It is so much safer to hope that the oats in your shed are good enough and everything will be OK. With that choice, sure, we can plant mostly good grain, but we also are planting weed seed that will inhibit the growth of what we cherish.

Whether work-related or personal, the heart of this journey in life is about connections. Modern psychology research tells us that the primary indicator of happiness in life is the quality of our social connections—relationships that are not just magically perfect from inception and beyond. Most often both sides know there are issues that should be discussed and resolved. If they are not, the unspoken, the un-dealt-with, the unresolved—the figurative weeds grow. We don't imagine the best. We ponder the worst. Un-clarity leads to very dirty grain and very weedy fields that do not reach their potential.

Cranking the flywheel may never be "fun." I cannot promise you that you will find immediate joy in tough conversations, opening up that "can of worms" at work or entering into a space in life that challenges the safety net of telling yourself you are just living with the cards you are dealt, the seeds in your bucket. The same is true for those tedious work tasks that no one enjoys, but that are so critical to success.

I *can* promise you that cranking that flywheel will be rewarding. Authentically rewarding. I have been fortunate to work with teams, organizations and leaders from around the globe. There are numerous common threads that weave within those groups and individuals that are great and those that are failing—and the most powerful is the ability and desire to turn the flywheel and get dusty.

Doing the dirty, unrewarding tasks in life—that is what truly separates Greatness from Average; superior, high-functioning teams from those that win every now and then; relationships that can survive any obstacle from those that crumble at the first sign of adversity.

Find joy in getting dirty. Seek out the flywheel shaft and crank it. The result will be worth it.

David Swan

Education: B.A., St. Olaf College; M.A.T., University of Wisconsin-River Falls

Work: Founder and CEO since 1998 of The Champions Circle, which specializes in guiding Vision to Victory. Deliver energetic and engaging leadership, management, customer loyalty, sales and personal-development seminars to organizations of all sizes and to over 9,000 participants from around the globe.

Book: *Outliers* by Malcom Gladwell

Quote: There is no substitute for hard work.
—Thomas A. Edison

More: www.ChampionsCircle.com

Living Optimistically

Loren Swanson

Being an optimist is an interesting way of living one's life. I know, because I have done that and continue to do that. It is my optimism that enabled me to buy my first business. Without the energetic attitude that optimism brings, I don't believe it ever would have worked. I led a team of people in a wholesale distributing enterprise. We focused our attention on getting the job done with our optimism, and it worked. That being said, there were times when my optimism got me in trouble, e.g., when I extended credit to some of the wrong people and got burned.

After that, I learned to listen to some of the others in the organization, and when I came in with the biggest order in the history of the company, the bookkeeper/accountant just smiled and said, "How's his credit?" I think President Reagan had it right when he said, "Trust but verify!"

Optimism is indeed a good trait and it will enable many things to happen that would not have happened otherwise. At the same time, like the rest of life, it must be in balance with all the other aspects of life.

I recently was talking with a client from the past and a video I had recorded with our Optimist Club was appropriate to the conversation. I sent him a link to the video with the Optimist Club credits and he responded very quickly, "Now

I understand why you are so optimistic!" His was a tough case and I remained optimistic for the three years it took to get the job completed. Without the optimism and the accompanying energy, it all would have died multiple times, but the optimism was what brought the success.

I have seen the upsides and downsides of optimism and have consciously decided that in my life, I'll exercise some caution and then accept the downsides of optimism as part of the process because the upsides of an optimistic attitude make my life far better overall.

Loren Swanson

Education: I've touched a lot of hot stoves! B.A., speech and philosophy, University of Minnesota; AFTCO training in practice transitions, transition management; Dale Carnegie course in human relations

Work: Senior transition analyst, AFTCO. Many transitions in MN, IA, ND, WI, and FL; president and CEO, Eames Distributing Co., Inc.; president and CEO, M. L. Sales Inc.; vice president, Elitecard Corporation. Licensed in real estate in Minnesota, Wisconsin, South Dakota, Colorado. Pilot of airplanes, gliders and hot air balloons.

Book: *The Wright Brothers* by David McCullough

Quote: The harder I work the luckier I get! —Anonymous

If At First You Don't Succeed, Try, Try Again

Scott D. Thomas

I have learned that nothing is easy and that we seldom succeed during our first try. We need to keep at it and eventually, success will find its way into our lives. Things do get easier as life progresses, and we master our craft. The answers have more clarity as we become wiser. However, we do need to keep searching for the answers to find clarity. Pushing forward and being all in and fully committed has been rewarding and recognized. Keeping at it has been rewarding on many levels. Having confidence in one's abilities and advocating one's skill sets is also important to move in a positive direction.

My profession as a mechanical consulting engineer for building systems has become more valued as developers and owners realize the impact that these systems have on the building's operating costs and life cycle.

I like to think that I come from humble beginnings. I never knew my father. I was raised by a single mother and her mother who was also single. They were very different people, who showed me that hard work does pay off. I was always motivated to work hard and make money from an early age. It was common to go without some of the luxuries that my peers were able to enjoy. My first job was as a paperboy in central Wisconsin, delivering papers in rain, sleet, snow and hot weather. I remember thinking that being a paperboy was more difficult than delivering mail since we had to deliver on foot and did not have a vehicle in which to drive around. Summers weren't bad since we could ride our bikes, but winters were difficult with snow, extreme cold conditions and early nightfall.

During high school, I worked at Hardee's about 30 hours per week. Many friends teased me about working fast food, but I always had money in my pocket and did not need to borrow money for necessities. I also worked fast food when I started going to college.

I got my first drafting job after my sophomore year of college, drafting HVAC (heating, ventilating and air conditioning) systems. During spring break of my sophomore year, my friends went to Florida and I went looking for a job. During a blizzard, I pounded the pavement, stopping in at engineering firms, seeking employment.

The company that hired me was very impressed with that type of fortitude and offered me a job. I kept at the drafting while attending college my junior and senior years. I also was a farm hand during the summer. I would go to my drafting job during the day and do farm work at night and weekends. Money was tight, and I needed to work as much as possible to make ends meet. Milwaukee School of Engineering is a private university and wasn't cheap. Financial aid was very helpful, but I still needed to work as much as possible. Pay was minimal since the economy was not in the best of shape. I graduated high school in 1980 and graduated college in 1984. I got married two weeks after graduating from college.

I have been married for 34 years. My wife's family has been an excellent example of what it means to take care of family and to work together. They are a very close-knit group of Polish, Norwegian and German heritage that has a strong work ethic and family values. They require a job well done. Mediocrity is not acceptable.

My wife and I are very different. They say opposites attract. We complement each other in many ways. She is more sociable than I am, and I take care of the numbers/financial planning. We always work together with major decisions and both provide excellent input and feedback to each other in each other's realm of expertise.

My wife is a school psychologist. Her career of choice required seven years of college education with a three-year master's degree that she pursued during our first four years of marriage. Upon completion of her degree, we moved from Milwaukee to the Twin Cities area to allow my wife to get a job in her field of choice. It was one of the best things we ever did. The economy in the Twin Cities has been very strong, which is important for my career.

I feel that I am truly blessed. Without optimism and faith in myself and others around me, my blessings would not be as great or significant. Personal development and a constant thirst for new knowledge has helped me to excel in my field and to become the leader that I am.

I am a second-generation owner of a consulting engineering firm that was founded in 1983. I started working there in 1991 and started purchasing stock in 1996. The company name is Cain Thomas Associates, Inc. The firm used to be Cain Ouse Associates, Inc. We changed the name in 2011 to more accurately reflect the current ownership of the company.

Running a company requires that you develop your leadership skills and rely on others around you. I have been focused on leadership development for approximately ten years. Leadership requires a service mindset in which the leader provides service to the company, employees and clients. Developing leadership skills has also developed emotional intelligence, providing better service to clients as well as employees. Leadership development is like exercise and brushing your teeth. You need to do it often to keep it in the forefront of your mind, so you can be the best leader possible. It is not about me; it is about the greater group around me. If we win as a team, the rewards will be greater for me as an individual.

My recent technical endeavors included obtaining a Master of Engineering in Fire Protection Engineering from the University of Maryland via an online education program. I also recently took the Professional Engineer exam and passed the exam, so I am now also a licensed Fire Protection Engineer in addition to being a licensed mechanical engineer. In addition to enhancing my knowledge about Fire Protection Engineering, the program also helped me to focus more intensely on technical subject matter and thus hone my technical skills and critical thinking.

I also obtained my LEED accreditation approximately ten years ago. LEED stands for Leadership in Energy and Environmental Design. This is very important to me because it shows a commitment to sustainable and energy-efficient design. From a young age, I have had a desire to help reduce our energy footprint in our engineering designs. LEED and sustainable design provides benchmarking and helps give these concepts a high priority. We all have an impact on our environment. The desire for sustainability is to leave our planet better than when we came.

I have three grown children ages 28 and 26—a daughter and twin sons. I am very proud that we have taught our children to be self-sufficient and not be dependent on their parents.

Give a man a meal and he will be hungry tomorrow. Teach a man to fish and he will never go hungry.

Scott D. Thomas

Education: B.S., architectural engineering from the Milwaukee School of Engineering; Master of Engineering in Fire Protection Engineering from the University of Maryland

Work: Owner and a principal mechanical engineer with Cain Thomas Associates and have worked for the company since 1991. I have been an engineer designing building systems since 1984.

Book: *True North* by Bill George

Quote: It's the little details that are vital. Little things make big things happen. —John Wooden

More: www.CTAMEP.com

www.linkedin.com/company/cain-thomas-associates-inc-/

My Story

Roger Williams

I believe there is a fine line between optimism, confidence and arrogance in approaching life's challenges. It is up to each of us to consider which of these is fueling our actions.

I've been extremely fortunate to have held a number of positions that required work that I had not previously performed, and in some cases had not been performed by anyone in the organization. While each of these opportunities were approached with a degree of caution and trepidation, there was also a feeling that a job could be accomplished with optimism and a sense of purpose.

I graduated from Iowa State University with a degree in landscape architecture in 1960. Following a two-year stint in the Army, I joined a multi-disciplinary design firm located in Duluth. It was my first real job. The firm had done work in Hoyt Lakes, Minnesota, for several years and, based on our performance, was asked if we could design a nine-hole golf course. The job fell to me. Recognizing that I hadn't golfed since high school and did not own a set of clubs, the assignment was overwhelming. I proceeded with more optimism than confidence, spending many hours researching golf course architecture and learning how to make a course both challenging and enjoyable for residents with various levels of proficiency.

With sound advice and support from others, the course was designed and literally carved from the wilderness with chainsaws and DuPont blasting powder. In 1966, long before the course was completed, I left the firm for a position with the State of Minnesota in St. Paul. One of my bucket-list items was to one day return to Hoyt Lakes and visit the completed course. On a fine day in June 2015, my daughter and I headed out to Hoyt Lakes. It was a weekday and not many players were on the course, giving us a fine opportunity to walk the fairways without bothering players. With a feeling of relief, I liked what I saw. But better yet, I spoke with players and maintenance personnel. They all spoke highly of the course and said it was a major attraction in the area and was well used. As we headed home, I remembered the days and nights I spent optimistically designing what I hoped would be a success.

It was optimism that guided me in leading other first-time projects. For example, in the late 1960s, a national park was proposed for the northern Minnesota boundary. It was very controversial, with economic and political forces taking sides along with residents of the state. Newly elected Governor Harold LeVander was neutral on the park and asked the Department of Natural Resources (DNR) to prepare a report on its pro's and con's. I was fortunate in being selected to work with a forester from the DNR to prepare the report. Based on its findings, the governor supported the proposal and formed an advisory committee of his commissioners. I was appointed to serve as its coordinator—a position that became the "public face" of the administration's quest for the park and, as such, absorbed both praise and criticism.

I worked closely with the state agencies, National Park Service, citizens organizations for and against the proposal, and members of Congress. Given the bitter rivalry between sides and great uncertainty as to Congress' intentions, it was literally optimism that kept the movement going forward. Finally, in 1969, a bill creating Voyageurs National Park was passed and signed by the President.

One day in 1985, I was met in the hallway by my commissioner of the state planning agency. He asked if I wanted a new assignment—providing mediation services to public agencies to help settle disputes and avoid going to court. I knew little about mediation but was ready for a change and accepted the challenge. After attending a 40-hour professional course in mediation and receiving lots of help, advice, and training from non-profit mediation organizations, the Minnesota Office of Dispute Resolution opened for business. I was optimistic that the office could be useful if only those agencies engaged in a dispute would trust the process.

We became the fifth state office of dispute resolution in the United States and during the next 15 years, my staff and I mediated hundreds of disputes involving special education, civil and human rights, and public policy, saving millions of dollars in legal fees. We also trained hundreds of public employees from all levels of government in conflict resolution. What started as an idea, grew into an institution that continues today.

Most of my work career, as well as 12 years on a city council, has involved controversy with those content with, and often benefiting from, the status quo. My point in sharing these examples is not to toot my own horn, but to demonstrate the new and exciting challenges that confront you if you are willing to rise to the occasion. There are endless possibilities that exist for meaningful progress and change if we do so with a well-thought-out sense of purpose, collaboration, and optimism in believing the task can and should be done.

Roger Williams

Education: B.S., Iowa State University, Ames, Iowa, landscape architecture and urban planning

Employment: State of Minnesota—33 years. Various agencies.

Book: *Little Fires Everywhere* by Celeste Ng

Quote: The greatest pleasure in life is doing what people say you cannot do. —Walter Bagehot

Peace begins with a smile.
MOTHER TERESA

Advice to Young Adults

Ben Withhart

The best advice I can offer is three-fold. One, always be kind, even when others spew anger or hatred. Two, believe in yourself. Take the risk. The old saying, "Nothing ventured, nothing gained" is true. Risks always pay off, sometimes as learning experiences making you a more knowledgeable individual. Three, try very hard to understand opposing viewpoints. Learn how to express them and the arguments that support that viewpoint that is opposite of your own.

Seek and create leadership opportunities. As a high school student, I practiced hard to win the solo trumpet chair in the band. I used this position to organize and lead two other musical groups—a stage band and a small Dixieland band that won a talent contest on local TV.

My true passion was sports, especially football. Due to a bad lawn mower accident at the end of 5th grade, I didn't walk without crutches until 9th grade. It was easier to run than walk, so I joined the track team. Football had to wait until my junior and senior years. I played fullback and defensive end on winning teams.

I attended college at Winona State University, playing football for two years. It was there I decided to change my major from history to park and recreation administration. I wanted to attend the University of Minnesota. However, they required you to start in the program as a freshman unless you were a transfer student from a similar program. So, I transferred to Southern Illinois University and was accepted into their program. The next quarter I transferred to the University of Minnesota. While I attended the University of Minnesota, I worked as a camp director for the Boys Clubs of Minneapolis—a great opportunity to hire and supervise staff.

After graduation, I accepted a job as the first director of the Hennepin County Retired Senior Volunteer Program (RSVP). I had to organize the program by recruiting volunteers and finding places for them to volunteer as well as working with an advisory committee. This was a terrific learning experience as there were many opportunities to take risks and learn.

Two years later I accepted a job as senior program director with Suburban Community Services, a United Way-supported agency. In three years I was promoted to social services director (elderly, mentally retarded and physically challenged services). At the age of 30 I became the youngest executive director and CEO in the history of the organization. I remained there until retirement. During that time I focused the mission on elderly only and changed the name of the agency to Senior Community Services. We started with a dozen staff and fewer than 100 volunteers. By my retirement, we had 180-plus staff, 5,000 volunteers, an $8 million budget, and were serving 15,000 elders and their families.

My public-services career began at age 21 when I successfully ran for a seat on the Mound City Council. At age 30 I ran unsuccessfully for State Senate, attended grad school at the University of Minnesota, and got married. Six years later found me living in Shoreview with a young family. I was asked to chair a successful bond-issue campaign that provided funds for a new city hall, community center, park improvements, and a city-wide trail system. That fall I ran for the Shoreview City Council and served seven terms with a six-year break to become a Boy Scout leader and youth football coach while all that time remaining involved on the city planning commission.

Always be kind. Understand others' point of view. Take risks.

Ben Withhart

Education: B.S., park and rec administration, University of Minnesota; masters program, Community Education, University of Minnesota; Mini MBA, St. Thomas University

Work: Executive director and CEO of Senior Community Services; president of the Council of Agency Executives; founder and board chair of Elder Partners (Volunteers of America, Catholic Charities, Wilder Foundation, Human Services Incorporated of Washington County, DARTS, and Senior Community Services); founder, Suburban Hennepin Community Action; founder, Metro Meals on Wheels; chair, MN Legislative Commission (larger suburbs); founder, Minnesota Park Foundation; founder, Shoreview Community Foundation.

Book: *Grant* and *Alexander Hamilton* by Ron Chernow

Quote: God, let me be the man my dog thinks I am.
—Anonymous

Life Lessons From My Sister: Despair to Delight (Then Do It Again)

Warren Wolfe

I am basically a glass-half-full guy. I expect things to turn out well, people to try their best. At times I suspect I'm a bit of a Pollyanna that way. But there are times when the shortcomings and darkness of the world roll over me—big things and little things.

Whenever I feel down or discouraged—you know, the weather, politics, strife in Syria, potholes, trout aren't biting, politics, arthritic knees, politics—there's one place I can turn to get my head straight: My youngest sister.

After all, while there's a lot wrong with the world, there's also a lot that's right.

My sister, now 57, has had multiple sclerosis since she was 21, about to graduate from college. Soon after she married her high school sweetheart and had a child years later (now a junior at St. Kate's), my sister has slowly seen her physical abilities decline.

During that time, my sister has worked at a nursing home, a computer company, a child-care network and her own web-page development company. She is an artist and writer, has written two books and maintains a monthly newsletter about creativity, spirituality and chronic illness.

In addition to conversations with her, it's Kate's

newsletter—*JourneyDancing, Kind Promises to Befriend Your Life*—
that helps me walk up to the precipice of despair, then back
into the light.

For if there ever was a person who demonstrates the true
nature of optimism—not ducking the darkness but working through it and returning to the reality of this miraculous
world—it's my sister Kate.

Even as a child she was a creative and amazingly perceptive
person. She was writing and putting on plays with neighborhood children when she was nine. I remember walking in
the park with her when she was 12 and I was 25 and going
through a divorce. Much more than my parents, she seemed
to understand my pain and embarrassment as the first (and
it turns out only) one in my family to be divorced.

Kate's journey with MS has been years of learning how to
cope with physical loss—from using a cane, to a walker, to an
electric scooter and now to an electric wheelchair. She uses
a computer to write and paint brushes to make beautiful art.

But now, with no movement in her right arm and almost
none in her left, she uses voice-activated software to write, a
computer mouse controlled by head movements, and a pencil
or paintbrush held in her mouth to make art. Recently, she
began using chin controls to operate her wheelchair.

It's a journey that would have led me to deep despair—a
place she knows well and visits from time to time. But she has
learned to walk that pathway—valley of the shadow of death?
That will be the inevitable destination with an incurable and
progressive disease.

She does it with eyes wide open, aware of and naming the
demons that rise up in the dark. She lives with the fear, anger,
despair and self-doubts. Then, slowly, she begins to adapt,
to see and accept the reality of what is, the new losses in

ability—even to rejoice in the new normal.

Then another change, another dance with the darkness. There is no shortcut; she can't escape the demons (*Dancing with Monsters: Chronic Illness as Creative Transformation* is the title of her first book).

It might be easy to say, "Well, sure, might as well make the best of what you have. What choice is there?"

Kate sees that at work, too, but that is not her resting place. She is determined to continue interacting with life fully, to delight in the people, sights, sounds, smells and tastes (it's not a peanut butter sandwich without dill pickle slices) that appear every day, every hour.

Two aides help her morning and night with her personal cares and getting in and out of her wheelchair. They and family members feed her. Her transportation comes from Metro Mobility or family members driving their accessible van.

But she remains passionately connected with people. In addition to her newsletter, she helps lead a discussion group for people with disabilities; conducts workshops on journaling for people with disabilities; attends church regularly; takes online courses in mediation, mindfulness and writing.

Until a few months ago, when weakness in her left hand no longer made steering her wheelchair safe, she volunteered weekly as an ESL instructor. Last summer she led a church committee investigating solar energy, and before that was a "friendly visitor" Stephen Minister at her church and served on its ruling body.

Her hope is to be able to remain living with her family at least until her daughter graduates from college in 2020 before her increasing physical needs mean she must move to a group home of some sort.

My lesson from Kate is not simply to say to myself, "Well,

I could have it a lot worse." Every person alive could have it a lot worse.

No, my lesson is that I have it even better than I realize, and that by paying attention, by opening my senses and rejoicing in what I find, I can live a more complete and fulfilling life.

And when I do that, I can enrich the lives of those around me—people I love, people I care about, even people I've never met as I learn to appreciate and celebrate the uniqueness of life.

Kate has taught me that the pathway to joy is just that—a path and not a destination.

I end with a nugget from Kate's March newsletter at http://www.journeydancing.com/:

Find Joy in the Present Moment:

What brings you delight? Watch for the moment when your heart lightens, the corners of your mouth turn up or you laugh out loud. Make a note of that moment in your journal each day. This occupies your mind with what psychologists call "positive scanning."

Warren Wolfe

Education: B.A., journalism and political science, University of Wisconsin-River Falls

Work: Reporter and news editor, *Red Wing Republican Eagle*; copy editor, reporter, assistant city editor, Minneapolis *StarTribune*.

Book: *The Silk Roads: A New History of the World* by Peter Frankopan

Quote: When one door of happiness closes, another opens; but often we look so long at the closed door that we do not see the one which has been opened for us. —Helen Keller

Driving By

Roger Worner

One Christmastime several years ago, I returned home to small-town North Dakota to spend a day and evening with my parents, both in the autumn of their lives. Simultaneously, my wife traveled on a similar mission to visit her aging parents in Iowa. The two of us had enjoyed our holiday a weekend earlier with our children, their spouses, and a burgeoning number of grandchildren, so we were free to fulfill our son/daughter obligations without fear of disappointing any of our loved ones.

It was not long into my visit that I detected a sadness in Dad that, quite frankly, was uncharacteristic of him. I asked if there were something wrong. He responded, "I guess I'm just thinking…about having lost two of my close friends this year." "Really!" I said. "I didn't know that. I'm sorry. Who were they?" My inquiry was sincere; I really did care, but I thought it highly improbable—not having lived in my hometown for 30 years—that I would even know the close friends he was about to mention. "Merritt Flynn and …" I never heard the second name, so fixated was I on learning that this man had passed away.

Merritt Flynn was a giant in my life. He was a professor of educational administration at North Dakota State University, advisor in my master's degree work, later an advocate of staggering proportions for me, and a friend. As it turned out, he was also my dad's friend, that having occurred when Dad received a vocational rehabilitation grant to leave the private sector to attend NDSU and complete an undergraduate degree he had begun but been forced—for financial reasons—to withdraw from the University of North Dakota during the years of the Great Depression. For two years, Dad and I, indeed, were college mates together, and a number of professors I had had as an undergraduate he in turn was meeting. Merritt Flynn was one of those professors, and, similar in age, they became fast friends. So, when Dad mentioned Merritt Flynn, my heart sank. I was saddened, but even more so I was pitifully embarrassed. Let me continue.

Upon completion of my program of studies, I landed my first teaching job in a tiny South Dakota school district as a mathematics and science teacher. Periodically, I'd stop by and visit Merritt at his home in Fargo. On a few occasions, we hunted ducks or pheasants together, eating field snacks his wife, Audrey, fixed for us. They were veritable feasts. Such nice, nice, nice people.

Then, returning home from teaching one day, there was a particular piece of mail that gave me momentary amusement. Of all things, Merritt had enclosed in an envelope an inexpertly typed copy of a letter to New York University he had written, advocating that I be considered for one of that institution's elite two-year doctoral fellowships. I felt such gratitude. I also pitied Merritt for his naiveté "How could he believe ...?!"

Six months later, the fellowship was mine, and I was attending my first summer classes at New York University.

The years passed rapidly. I completed my doctorate, thrice became an assistant superintendent, twice a superintendent and, then, a consultant to hundreds of far-flung school districts.

I periodically kept in touch with Merritt, though not really very much. He retired. He and Audrey aged. Their son moved far away, so they saw less of him. Then Audrey died and, later, Merritt moved to a care center in Fargo.

I was undertaking many consulting studies in North Dakota and western Minnesota in Audrey's and Merritt's waning years. Opportunities abounded for me to stop by but I didn't. I wanted to, I thought I'd do it next time, I thought Next time, Next time, Next time. Next time I didn't, I didn't, I didn't. Too late!

"I lost two of my close friends this year. Merritt Flynn ...," Dad said.

"Oh, God, why did I not stop by many times or even one last time to see you in that nursing home ... to hold your hand... and thank you one more time ... and to say, 'I love you, Pal.'?" I could have so easily done so.

On that drive home at Christmastime, I was haunted by my failures and, indeed, all of our failures. I was, and continue to be, resolved that I'm done "driving by." Now, in the twilight of my life, I am all the more convicted of my responsibility to stop by, call, write, extend a caring, loving word to those who have played any role in my life. If I fail to do so, most assuredly the opportunity will slip away. And that would be sad. I know it from experience.

Roger Worner

Education: B.A. and M.S., North Dakota State University; Ph.D., New York University

Work: My career has had three facets. Assistant superintendent *and* superintendent of schools; consultant (to school districts); education professor at St. Cloud State University. My superintendencies were in Mason City, IA, Roseville, MN, Glencoe-Silver Lake, MN, and Centennial (Lino Lakes), MN.

Book: *On Emotional Intelligence*, published by Harvard Business Review Press

Quote: For God so loved the world, He gave his only begotten Son that whosoever believes in Him will have everlasting life. — John 3:16

You are never too old to set another goal
or to dream a new dream.

C.S. LEWIS

The Fortunate Fly

Mary Kay Ziniewicz

About 15 years ago, I had an idea for a magazine. The idea was to showcase wisdom gained from living, with content supplied by those who walked before me, and shared with those seeking guidance in life on relationships, career, finances, spirituality, etc.—people like me.

The inspiration for the magazine that I called *Tyro* was my mentor, Linda. Linda is 25 years my senior, and she was my supervisor at an advertising agency. I thought Linda was brilliant, and Linda thought I was brilliant, too! No wonder we got along so famously!! Linda was (and still is) one of my favorite people and my biggest fan—actually, my only fan for a long time, to tell you the truth.

Linda would give me one piece of advice on a regular basis, "Mary Kay, you can catch more flies with honey." My response was always the same, "Linda, I don't want to hang around a bunch of flies!" Linda would laugh, because Linda thought I was clever and funny. Most everyone else saw me as aggressive, pushy, self centered, and probably rude, too. Yes, I was described as walking to the beat of a different drummer and I was referred to as a steamroller (and no doubt worse) by colleagues. In my mind, messages such as these meant that I wasn't ordinary (like them) and that I got things done (unlike them).

In my career, I was gaining ground, and that is what mattered most to me at the time—not what others thought or even how I treated them. I moved on from working at the advertising agency and I was leading marketing strategy for a law firm. I was happy because I wrote the marketing plan and executed the plan—my way—no team involved.

During my first year with the law firm, I wrote a plan and executed the plan exactly as I had envisioned. Success!

At the end of that first year, I received reviews from 30 lawyers at the law firm. Not mincing words, the lawyers told me that I did a lousy job. They said that I didn't know who they were and as a result, the work I produced was not reflective of them. I was not happy. In fact, I was angry. Immediately, I thought … I'm leaving this firm as soon as I can find another, better job.

The same week that I read the reviews (no lie), I received a phone call from the *Star Tribune*. A business reporter wanted to feature my firm and my work on the front page of the business section. Then another call came in. This time it was an editor of an international legal publication. The editor asked me to submit a story about the groundbreaking work that I spearheaded at the modest-sized firm in the Twin Cities. Needless to say, I felt accomplished. Clearly, the lawyers did not know what they were talking about. I was right, they were wrong. Ha!

Shortly after the media accolades, the managing partner of the firm and I traveled to a conference together. I thought he would tell me how sorry he was about the reviews and how his partners don't know much about marketing … but he did not. Instead, he said, "Five partners are turning 50 this year and I'd like you to plan a birthday party. And, by the way, I'm turning 50 and I want this to be a surprise."

Oh my! I was horrified. How dare he ask me, the most celebrated marketing director, to plan a birthday party? My response was, "Okay." But I was burning inside. I was determined to leave the firm. But until I found a new job, I needed to plan this party. So the planning began.

I proceeded to plan a birthday party for five attorneys who were turning 50. I figured out what I was going to do right away. The plan was to put together a photo video of the lawyers, including each decade of each of their privileged lives, slap down time-appropriate music, fill in historical happenings, and bam, the gift would be done.

To get their photos, I arranged meetings with their significant others—spouses, kids, parents. As I met with their families, I heard wonderful stories about the attorneys—stories about their dreams, their accomplishments, their children, their sacrifices, their losses, their happiest and proudest days, and their sad days, too. I learned about them—who they were—kind, loving, smart people. And I learned about who they are now as they neared 50. I liked them. I related to them.

So one day, as I was relaxing on my deck reading a *Vanity Fair* magazine, I read an article about the Ralph Lauren car exhibit at the Boston Museum of Art. Immediately I thought about Howard—one of the attorneys being celebrated who happened to be my boss. Howard loves fashion. He loves fancy cars. And he loves Boston. So I picked up the phone and called the curator of the show. I knew his name from the article. I said something like, "I'm calling for an unusual purpose. I am looking for a gift to give an attorney who is turning 50. I read about your show, and I'm wondering if you might have an idea for a gift. The curator, who was so happy that I was excited about his show, offered to give Howard and his wife a private, after-hours, tour of the show. For free.

I couldn't believe how willing someone was to do something so thoughtful for someone (a lawyer!) they didn't know. This formula was repeated to create four more wonderful experiences, including throwing the first pitch at a Saints game, submitting art for the Art in Bloom show at the Minneapolis Institute of Art, a feature story in Surdyk's wine magazine with a wine-maker client, and attending Ebertfest and meeting Roger Ebert!

Well, so the rest of the story is that the night the party finally came—the party took place in Las Vegas—the video played. People (all of the firm attorneys) loved it. Then I surprised each of them with their own personal experience. Tears were shed. Yes, attorneys cry. I saw them.

We all grew. The night was magical. We learned about one another. The lawyers learned about their partners. I learned that I really liked being around these beautiful people.

The experience was life-changing for me. From that time forward, I focused on making others shine and letting them know they mattered to me. My career soared from that moment because I earned the trust of my colleagues. I was catching flies with honey and loving every moment of being genuinely caring. I learned that I was fortunate if the flies wanted to hang out with me.

As for the magazine *Tyro*, I had the opportunity to pitch the magazine concept to *Time* magazine in 2003. At that time, the concept did not fit in with the publication-buyer market. I believe today it would be different. And that is why I am so excited about the Optimist Club initiative. Great idea!

Mary Kay Ziniewicz

Education: B.A., mass-media communication, University of Akron, Akron, Ohio

Work: First job was delivering *The Cleveland Press* at age 6! Founder, Horse's Mouth Creative, LLC, 2009-present; director of marketing and business development at Barnes and Thornberg (formerly Parsinen Kaplan Rosberg & Gotlieb, P.A.); chief marketing officer, Gurstel Chargo, P.A.

Book: *The War That Saved My Life* by Kimberly Brubaker Bradley

Quote: For my thoughts are not your thoughts, neither are your ways my ways, declares the Lord. As the heavens are higher than the earth, so are my ways higher than your ways and my thoughts than your thoughts. —Isaiah 55: 8-9

More: https://www.linkedin.com/in/mziniewicz/

An optimist is someone who goes after Moby Dick in a rowboat and takes the tartar sauce with him.

ZIG ZIGLAR

Acknowledgments

Optimist International for their dedication to the development of youth, their communities, and themselves.

Don Salverda, founder and first president of the Roseville Area Optimist Club, Roseville, Minnesota. Don believed in this book from the initial idea, suggested including a photo with each story, and made the book possible through his wise counsel, proofreading, and phone calls.

Zola Burns, club treasurer and administrator—and eagle-eyed proofreader!—for willingly adding book-related activities to an already demanding list of club-related responsibilities.

Dave Schaps, club secretary, for developing the publisher agreement that put our book and its contributors on solid legal ground, for sending extra book-related emails, and for being steadfastly enthusiastic about the book from the start.

Club board of directors for support and guidance for this adventurous project.

Speakers for generously sharing their perspective, wisdom, and expertise.

Club members for contributing their stories that will be meaningful and enriching for readers at all stages of their own lives.

Terra Rathai for donating her photos and accompanying quotes for the section-divider pages. avantgardenstudio.com

Debra Kass Orenstein, copyright attorney, for valuable advice on the "fair use" of copyrighted material.

VOICES

OF

OPTIMISM

ROSEVILLE AREA OPTIMIST CLUB

ROSEVILLE, MINNESOTA

ISBN: 978-1-7321973-5-0
eISBN: 978-1-7321973-6-7

Printed in the United States of America by Bookmobile.
First edition.

Divider-page photo artworks donated by Terra Rathai,
Avant Garden Studio, www.avantgardenstudio.com

Editing, design, and cover photo donated by Sue Filbin.
(Quotes that fill spaces were selected and placed by the editor, not the authors.)

For information about *Voices of Optimism*,
or the Roseville Area Optimist Club,
please visit our website: www.rosevilleareaoptimistclub.com